SILAS WALTER ADAMS

THE LEGALIZED CRIME OF BANKING

AND A CONSTITUTIONAL REMEDY

ⒸMNIA VERITAS

SILAS WALTER ADAMS

THE LEGALIZED CRIME OF BANKING
& A CONSTITUTIONAL REMEDY

First Edition – 1958

Published by Omnia Veritas Ltd

ⓈMNIA VERITAS

www.omnia-veritas.com

TABLE OF CONTENTS

*T*he *Legalized Crime of Banking* is a simple story of The Federal Reserve System, dealing principally with the unconstitutional creation of money and the control of credit by private corporations. The author suggests a concrete, simple solution, which Congress could employ, which would make the transition from private banking to the Treasury without injuring anyone enjoying a constitutional right, or without upsetting our normal course of trade, industry, and agriculture.

THE PAUPER AND THE RICH MAN

The pauper (the Federal Reserve Bank) with assets of $52 billion with no productive know how, and less than 100,000 stockholders, loaned the rich man (The United States Government) with well over $350 billion in physical assets plus $250 billion in productive capacity and know how, with 170 million stockholders, $300 billion to fight World War II. Can you imagine the greatest corporation on earth, with 170 million stockholders and assets running over $600 billion, turning to a corporation with less than 100,000 stockholders and assets of only $52 billion to borrow money? Can you imagine Rockefeller saying to his chauffer: "Tom, I am transferring my personal chequeing account, which is around $1 billion, to your account; you may spend it as you please, provided that when I need some cash, you will hand it to me. Of course, I will give you my note for cash I receive and pay interest on the note." Well, that is exactly what Congress did in 1913 when it passed the Reserve Act. To fight World War II, we gave the bankers of the United States $300 billion in U.S. Bonds that we might use the Nation's credit.

In addition, we permitted them to take a credit of $300 billion in their reserve accounts. This gave them $2 trillion 100 billion bank credit. These credits are to bankers what your deposit credits on their books are to you. They can lend it, or buy investment obligations-it is cash to them! So adding the $300 billion in Bonds to their bank credit, we find that the bankers (the then paupers) came out of World War II $2 trillion 400 billion richer than when we went into the War. The United States Government (the then rich man), thanks to the stupidity and venality of her sons (congressmen), and newspapers and journals, came out of the War $300 billion in debt! And, dear reader, that fable happens to be true.

Who has dared to publish challenging books on money, exemplifying those qualities of rugged and courageous man hood so essential in the ongoing of a free republic, in which no man should be afraid to speak when he feels it his duty to speak. He has spoken through the many books which he has published, proving that a free press, in his opinion, is the guardian genius of a just, honest, and humane democracy. He has felt with Lincoln that "To sin by silence when they know they should protest, makes cowards of men." In appreciation of him as a publisher, I dedicate this book.

The Author.

To My Banker Acquaintances

I have assailed you in much harsher terms than I do
when I think of you as my neighbour. I don't think that
you ever stopped to analyse what you are really doing in
your banking business. I think you are a gambler at
heart, and gamblers have big hearts — Al Capone took
from the rich and ministered to the poor; so did Robin
Hood — only, dear sirs, you don't minister to the poor.
Many of you have never reasoned that you are the
croupiers at the roulette tables, and have been taught
that it is part of the game to press your foot on the
hidden pedal just in time to win the table's take. Many
of you have been stepping on the pedal never knowing
that you did; because you were afraid to investigate,
fearing that you might find you conscience and streak
of honesty too big to let you keep walking on such
treacherous ground.

I know that you reason as my good banker friend in
Port Lavaca reasoned when he said to me: "You must
not forget that there is a great deal of difference
between a moral wrong and a legal right." And maybe
you have a true picture of banking and its evils, and say
with Sir Josiah Stamp, "... but as long as the nation will
let men do this thing, a man is foolish not to be a
banker."

I'd lay down my life for your right deeds; I would
sacrifice your good esteem that I might combat a
wrong.

I hope that within the immediate decade, you must cease forever to be bankers; and become what you stoutly maintain you are, "money lenders."

Yours with deep regret,

S.W. Adams.

What Is And What Might Have Been.

First memorize the succinct, beautifully worded Purposes of Our Government, the Preamble to the Constitution of the United States:

"We, the people of the United States, in order to form a more perfect Union, establish justice, insure domestic tranquillity, provide for the common defence, promote the general welfare, and secure the blessings of liberty to ourselves and our posterity, do ordain and establish this Constitution for the United States of America."

Under the Federal Reserve Banking System, World War II has cost us to date:

U.S. Bonds, a gift to bankers.	$250 billion
New customers' deposits ...	$250 billion
Created new bank credit a gift	$1,250 billion
Annual interest to date ...	$120 billion
Total	$1,870 billion

By 1980, another $130 billion in interest will make the cost of World War II exactly $2 trillion ($2,000,000,000,000).

Had Congress in 1933 taken over the creating of money and the keeping of the people's deposits, cashing and clearing our cheques, World War II would have cost us just $250,000,000,000 (billion). And to date that would have been a saving to the people of the stupendous sum of $1,620,000,000,000 (trillion).

And the costs for future wars, and they will always be the creatures of bankers, annually, will be $32 billion. This cost since World War II has approximately amounted to $384,000,000,000 (billion), which is more than the total wealth of the United States in 1932.

THE LEGALIZED CRIME OF BANKING

AND A CONSTITUTIONAL REMEDY

CHAPTER I

FOREWORD

Fifty-two years ago in August, 1905, I went to Abbott, Texas, as principal of the school. Later in the fall the little bank in West, Texas, seven miles away, failed.

This story was told to me: A farmer sold his farm for $3600 cash. He reached the bank as the cashier was closing the doors. The farmer said, "I have just sold my farm. Here are $3600 — all I own is in my hands. I am afraid to keep it until I go west and buy another farm. Will you open the bank, and let me deposit this money? I owe you $500. I will come in Monday and pay you."

"Sure," replied the young cashier. He reopened the doors, took the farmer's money, gave him a deposit slip, knowing that the bank was busted, and would not reopen, Monday. He stuck the money in his expensive pants pocket, closed the doors, and later boarded a train for Dallas, for a week-end of pleasure, as was the custom in those days.

He didn't open the bank on Monday. The bank later was opened, and the vault was clean of cash. A reward was offered for the cashier's arrest and return. A friend brought him in and they split the reward. The youth of the town met the train, and gave him an ovation. A "moot" court freed him.

Depositors lost all. The farmer lost his $3600. The bank went to the same court and got judgment against the farmer for the note plus interest and costs of court.

When I heard that story, and learned that the law permitted crooked bankers to close their doors, write off every deposit on their books, yet sue those same depositors, if they owed the bank, and get judgment; and the depositors could not sue the bankers and get judgment for the lost deposit- credits; not even when the depositor had put actual cash in the day before the bank closed, as had the farmer, I said to myself, the real me:

"I shall set myself to the task of learning how such a crime against decency, justice and equity could have the sanction of law: why a deposit slip has no standing in court, yet the note a man gave the bank for the deposit slip has; why a depositor cannot sue a busted bank on a deposit slip and get judgment against the stockholders of the bank, while the stockholders can sue and get judgment on the note the depositor gave the bankers in exchange for the deposit slip; why a banker could take a farmer's cash, his life's savings, and abscond legally, then sue the victim on his note and get judgment, yet the depositor had no recourse at law."

So for 52 years the practices of bankers have been deep in my subconscious mind. I have read everything that I could find on banking and money; scanned newspapers and magazines for revealing information. I found that all I read was coloured, or half told, that the people might be kept ignorant of money, banking. Bankers misinformed me as often as I asked them for information. I could only observe bankers in action, from the deposit-window point of view, and as a borrower.

A quarter of a century later I had the answer, but I still lacked official confirmation of my discoveries. On May 1, 1939, the Board of Governors of the Federal Reserve System published a booklet of 128 pages — "The Federal Reserve System — Its Purposes and Functions." I got hold of a copy. It officially confirmed the correctness of my findings.

The Constitution of the United States of America is explicit in its delegation of powers to Congress. It says:

"The Congress shall have power... to coin money, regulate the value thereof, and of foreign coin, and fix the standard of weights and measures."

After enumerating the legalized crimes of banking, and proving that the coining of money and credit can not be re-delegated to others, I shall outline the plan of returning to the Congress of the United States the creation of our money and the control of the Nation's credit. This charge will not be felt adversely by the honest, working citizen, and it will greatly improve our economic situation.

It will hurt bankers, stock market gamblers, those who live by their smartness. In the language of Sir Josiah Stamp, President of the Bank of England and the second richest man in the British Empire, as said in an informal talk to 150 University of Texas history, economics and social science professors, in the 20's.

"Banking was conceived in iniquity and born in sin... Bankers own the world. Take it away from them, but leave them the power to create money and control credit, and with a flick of the pen, they will create enough money to buy it back again... Take this power away from bankers, and all great fortunes like mine will disappear, and they ought to disappear, because this would then be a better and a happier world to live in... But if you want to continue to be the slaves of bankers, and pay the costs of your own slavery, let them continue to create money, and control credit."

Stop and find your place in our present economic system - that is, are you a beneficiary; or, are you a victim? Are you a gainer; or, are you a loser?

If you work for a living, with hands and/or head, or both; or, work for others for pay, you are a loser, the heaviest of all losers! You toil to provide man all his material wants, or to serve him, and you are paid with a cheap, inflated 25-cent dollar, which we persistently call a 100-cent dollar — a private dollar created by a private corporation. If you have earned your money either by producing something, working for yourself or as an employee, or in serving others, and through thrift and economy you have stored it away for the rainy day; or, if an honest man and would not take anything from another that you did not give in return an equal value of goods and/or service, you are doubly a loser; for the bankers' constant stream of created new dollars pouring into circulation cheapens your dollar, and lowers its buying power. You get only a pound of coffee today for the same money you could buy four pounds of coffee in the thirties.

If you are on a pension, or living on your life's saving, even on the coupons you have been clipping from World War II U.S. Bonds, you are a helpless loser, because bankers in the last 20 years have reduced the buying power of your dollar to one-fourth its 1935 buying power.

But, if you are a gambler, and live by your wits play the stock markets and otherwise take usury, take from others without producing or serving others, take that which you have not earned, you are a gainer; aye, more, an enemy of all honest, producing, serving, toiling people. You are the burden that is crushing to the earth the masses, the 99 and 9 of us.

Austin, Texas

The Author.

PREFACE

On July 4, 1951, I issued a little 16-page pamphlet, "The Legalized Crime of Banking - Facts About Money," and it slept peacefully in my office until on or about July 4, 1957. In some way an interest grew among the people, and now I am getting orders for it from coast to coast.

I am reproducing the major portion of that pamphlet, because it exposes the "Legalized Crime of Banking," in a nut shell. It is a thumb-nail story of the abuses of the bankers in their creation of money, and their control of the Nation's (not their own) credit.

I am giving you this story, because it covers the entire process of creating bank reserves, bank credit, and deposits to the credit of the people on the books of the 14,756 commercial banks in the United States.

You cannot refute, deny, or question this summary of the evils of banking, because I quote the Board of Governors to prove every statement I make. However, the booklet issued May, 1939, by the Board of Governors of the Federal Reserve System, cannot be had at this time at any price, unless you find it in some private library, and find the owner willing to sell. I have one, and no price would buy it, because after Mr. Eccles left the Board of Governors as chairman, everything that could be done, has been done to suppress the circulation of the book. They have reprinted some of it under a "revised" edition, and the same name, "The Federal Reserve System — Its Purposes and

Functions," but they studiously omitted all these damaging (to bankers) statements.

Because just a thumb-nail story never completed the task of informing the people and the creating in their minds a determination to do something about a situation, I shall go into repetitious details, and cite many instances of the practices of bankers, that you may know that indeed you are the slaves of the bankers, and "pay the cost of your own slavery."

After you have read this thumbnail story of banking, I am sure that you will want to know more about it; and what my solution of the problem is.

Note: My son's Publishing House, "The Chaparral Press," is reprinting this Reserve booklet, and you may get a copy on request, at a very nominal cost, through The Meador Publishing Company, 324 Newbury Street, Boston 15, Massachusetts, or directly from The Chaparral Press, 2004 South First, Austin 4, Texas.

The Author.

CHAPTER II

QUOTATIONS FROM THE BOOKLET

The Federal Reserve System — Its Purposes and Functions

Before we go into the discussion of the banking problem, I want to give you many quotations from the booklet issued May 1, 1939, by the Board of Governors of the Federal Reserve System, during the chairmanship of Marriner S. Eccles.

Page 18: "The Federal Reserve Open Market Committee comprises the seven members of the Board of Governors, and five representatives of the Federal Reserve Banks. The Committee directs the open market operations of the Federal Reserve Banks; that is, the purchases and sales of United States Government securities *and other obligations in the open market*."

Page 18: "Member banks include all national banks in the continental United States, and such State banks and Trust companies as apply for membership, meet the requirements, and are admitted. On December 31, 1938, the membership comprised 5,224 National banks and 1,114 State banks. There were over 8,000 other State banks and trust companies that did not belong to the system..."

Pages 19 & 20: " .. Currency is actually used for only a small part of the country's total volume of payments, the greater part being effected by the use of bank:

cheques... it is possible for them to borrow additional funds from their Federal Reserve Bank, and possible for the Federal Reserve authorities on their own initiative to supply additional funds *through open market purchases.*"

Page 22: "The Federal Reserve Act... empowered the Reserve authorities to discount paper for member banks, to engage in open market operations, and to issue Federal Reserve notes...

The *member banks... may deposit in their reserve accounts in Reserve Banks the cheques on other banks* (after first giving deposit credits to customers on the bank's book-double deposits) *and surplus currency received from their customers*, and on the other hand, they may draw on their reserve accounts for various purposes, especially to procure currency and to pay the cheques drawn on them by their customers and deposited in other banks."

Page 23: "Since the Federal Reserve authorities have the power to increase or decrease the supply of reserve funds and within limits to increase or decrease reserve requirements, they are able to exercise considerable influence over the amount of credit, in the aggregate, that banks may extend."

Pages 23-24: "The duties of the Reserve authorities ... are principally the following: hold member bank reserve balances; furnish currency for circulation; facilitate the clearance and collection of cheque; supervise member banks and obtaining reports from them; and act as fiscal agents, custodians, and depositories for the United States Government."

Page 26: "Federal Reserve notes are liabilities of the Federal Reserve Banks that issue them... They are also obligations of the United States Government." Which makes the Government the guarantor of private notes.

Page 26: "Treasury currency, comprising silver certificates, silver dollars, subsidiary silver, minor coin and United States notes, is issued by the Treasury itself, but it is placed in circulation ... through the Reserve Banks."

Page 27: "All United States paper currency is printed at the Bureau of Engraving and Printing in Washington, D.C., and all United States coins are made at the Philadelphia Denver and San Francisco mints ... operated by the United States Treasury. Federal Reserve Notes are printed by the Bureau at the expense (30 cents a $1,000) of the Federal Reserve Banks."

Page 27: "There are two principal ways by which any individual gets paper money and coin. Either he draws it out of his bank and has it charged to his account; or, he is paid for his labour, his services, or his merchandise with money that has been drawn out of a bank by someone else."

Page 28: "Banks provide themselves with the amounts and kinds of cash that the people want. Member banks depend upon the Federal Reserve Banks for replenishment of their supply, ordering what they require and having it charged to their reserve accounts. Non-member banks generally get their supply from member banks."

Pages 30-31: "The use of cheques is facilitated by the services of the Federal Reserve Banks in clearing and collecting them through the reserve accounts of member banks. For example, suppose a Hartford, Connecticut, manufacturer sells $1,000 worth of electrical supplies to a dealer in Sacramento California and receives a cheque on a bank in Sacramento... The Hartford manufacturer ... deposits the cheque in his Hartford bank. The Hartford bank does not require cash for the cheque; it wants credit in its reserve account at the Federal Reserve Bank of Boston. Accordingly, it sends the cheque to the Federal Reserve Bank of Boston (which credits Hartford banks reserve account $1,000). The Federal Reserve Bank of Boston sends it to the Federal Reserve Bank of San Francisco. The Federal Reserve Bank of San Francisco debits the Sacramento bank's reserve account $1,000 and sends it to the Sacramento bank. The bank in Sacramento charges the cheque account of the depositor (the electrical dealer) who wrote it, and either remits the amount to the Federal Reserve Bank of San Francisco or authorizes the San Francisco Reserve Bank to charge the amount to its reserve account. The Federal Reserve Bank in San Francisco thereupon credits the Federal Reserve Bank of Boston.

The Federal Reserve Bank of Boston in turn credits the account of the Hartford bank. Thus the cheque effects the transfer through the Federal Reserve Banks of $1,000 of deposit credit from the chequeing account of the dealer in Sacramento to the chequeing account of the manufacturer in Hartford and transfers $1,000 In Reserve from San Francisco Reserve bank to Boston Reserve Bank to credit of Sacramento bank."

Page 32: "Cheques which are collected and cleared through Federal Reserve Banks must be paid in full by the banks on which they are drawn, without deductions of a fee or charge." Page 35: "The twelve Federal Reserve Banks carry the principal chequeing accounts of the United States Treasury, handle much of the work entailed in issuing and redeeming Government Obligations, and perform numerous other fiscal duties of the United States Government."

Page 39 "The aggregate deposits in the banking system as a whole represent mainly funds lent by banks or paid by banks for securities, mortgages, and other forms of investment obligations. It may seem that it should be the other way around that bank loans and investments would be derived from bank deposits (to the credit of customers) instead of bank deposits being derived from loans and investments; and it is true that deposits would not grow out of loans if currency were to be used by the public for monetary payments to the exclusion of bank deposits transferable by cheque. But as it is, the public in general prefers to have its monetary funds — including what it borrows — on deposit in banks rather than in the form of currency in its own possession. The result of this preference is that the proceeds of loans go on deposit to be disbursed by cheques, and aggregate deposits are increased.

"Suppose for example, that a man borrowed $1,000 from a bank and took his loan in currency. The bank would have $1,000 less currency than before and in its place a promissory note for $1,000. Its deposits would remain unchanged. (But when others returned the cash for deposit new deposits would be created.) But suppose that the borrower, preferring not to take the currency, asked for $1,000 deposit credit instead, it (the bank) would have $1,000 more deposits (also the note) in its books. The loan instead of decreasing the bank's cash balance would have increased its deposits.

"Or suppose that the bank purchases a $1,000 Government bond from one of its customers. The customer does not want payment in currency — he wants payment in deposit credit.

Accordingly, the bank acquires a $1,000 bond and its deposits increased by $1,000. The bank's currency is not involved in the transaction and remains what it was.

"... when banks give deposit credits to their customers, they assume an obligation to pay the customers' cheques. Consequently, they must have funds on hand for the purpose; though ordinarily the amount need not be more than a (small) fraction of the total deposit liability." Foot Note, page 40: "As this and the preceding paragraphs indicate, a bank's purchases of investments, i.e., notes, bonds, mortgages, etc., is an extension of credit just as loans are; and bank investments increase bank deposits just as loans do. For the sake of simplicity, the terms 'lending and extension of credit' are often used where the purchase of the investments by banks as well as lending by banks is meant."

Page 42: "... member banks are required to maintain reserves of a certain volume with the Federal Reserve Banks, and at the same time the Federal Reserve Banks are given the power to advance additional reserve funds to them either by lending to them directly or by purchasing securities and other forms of (investment) obligations in the open market."

Page 44: "While maintaining his average reserve balance at or above the minimum requirement, a banker may make constant and active use of his reserve account. From day to day he may have credits to his account for cheques on other banks received from his depositors; and from day to day he may have charged to the account for cheques that have been drawn on him and deposited in other banks. He may also from time to time withdraw currency and have it charged to the account, and when he has more currency than he needs, he may deposit it at the Reserve bank to be credited to his account...

Suppose, for example, that a given bank has $2,000,000 of deposits, is required to have reserves of 10 percent, (of the $2 million) and has exactly that amount, namely $200,000. If a customer deposits an additional $100,000, either in cash or in the form of a cheque on another bank, the first bank not only has its deposits increased by that amount, but also is put in position to increase its reserves equally by depositing the currency or cheque in the Federal Reserve Bank." Page 45: "In brief, when borrowed funds are chequed out, the (page 46) result is a decrease in reserves; and when they remain on deposit, the result is an increase in deposits without an increase in reserves. In either event, lending has an immediate reaction upon the ratio of reserves to deposits. And, as a corollary, the amount of reserves held in relation to legal requirements is a controlling factor in the lending policy of a bank."

Page 48: "The loans which individual member banks may obtain from the Federal Reserve Banks are of two classes: (1) the discount of so-called eligible paper; and (2) advances.

Eligible paper consists principally of notes, drafts, and bills of exchange used to finance payments for agricultural and industrial products. Advances may be made by a Federal Reserve Bank to a member bank on the latter's promissory note secured by collateral. (Page 49) Under the two foregoing provisions a Federal Reserve Bank may supply a member bank with any amount of additional reserves the member bank needs, the only limitation being the amount of good assets the member bank can offer the Federal Reserve Bank as security."

Page 50: "In recent years, however, banks have had a large volume of excess reserves, there has been little occasion for them to borrow from Federal Reserve Banks." (Note: Sure: The $250 billion U.S. Bonds gave banks $1,250 billion Reserves.)

Page 50: "The second method of supplying banks with additional reserve funds is through open market purchases (Page 51) of government securities and other obligations. These purchases are undertaken at the initiative of the Federal Reserve authorities and not of individual member banks. They do not have particular banks in view, but the aggregate reserves of the banking system as a whole.

"Securities purchased by the Federal Reserve authorities in the open market come out of the portfolios either of banks themselves or of investors and corporations that are customers of banks. If they come out of the portfolios of investors and corporations, the cheques given in payment by the Federal Reserve authorities (Page 52) are deposited by the investor and the corporation in their respective banks" and as a result bank deposits are increased. The banks in turn deposit the Reserve authorities' cheque in their reserve accounts at the Federal Reserve Bank, so that reserves also are increased (dollar for dollar) purchases of securities by the Federal Reserve authorities always increase the reserves of banks, therefore open market purchases increase bank reserves relative to bank deposits, they tend to furnish member banks a larger basis for credit expansion... Thus if $100,000,000 of securities purchased by the Reserve authorities came from the portfolios of investors, the result would be that bank deposits as well as reserves would be increased by that amount."

Page 55: "Loans and purchases of securities by the Federal Reserve authorities are one of the important sources of member bank reserves; member bank reserves in turn are the basis of member bank credit-that is, of the loans and investment: of member banks. And member bank credit is a source of bank deposits transferable by cheque wherewith business men and other persons make the bulk of their monetary payments. ...

"In other words, member bank credit is used chiefly in the form of member bank deposits subject to cheque; Federal Reserve Bank credit is used chiefly in the form of member bank reserves held on deposit with the

Reserve Banks; and the volume of member bank reserves — deriving in greater or less degree from Federal Reserve Bank Credit (which is the Nation's credit subrogated to them by Congress, gratis. — The author) determines the ability of member (Page 56) banks to meet the demands of their borrowers for member bank credit.

"It is important to note, however, that Federal Reserve Bank credit and member bank credit are not the equivalent of each other, dollar for dollar. Member bank reserves do not have to be increased by $500 million of Federal Reserve bank credit in order to make possible an increase of $500 million in member bank credit. The additional Federal Reserve Bank credit needed will be only a fraction (1/5 on an average) of the additional member bank credit to be extended... "Suppose that banks were required to maintain reserves of 20 percent and that they had just that 20 percent and no more. Then if the deposits were to be increased by $500 million, they would have to increase their reserves by but $100,000,000. Accordingly, the $100 million of Federal Reserve Bank credit obtained by borrowing or by the sale of securities to the Federal Reserve Banks would increase their reserves sufficiently to enable them to expand their own credit by 500 million."

Page 68: "Bank deposits result chiefly from loans and other extension of credit by banks."

Page 69: "Suppose there were only one bank instead of several thousand, and that this one bank did all of the commercial banking business of the country. Suppose further that this bank were required by law to have reserves equal to at least 20 percent of its deposits. Thus if it had deposits of $5 billion, its reserve balance with the Reserve Bank would have to be at least $1 billion."

Page 70: "Suppose, however; that the Reserve authorities were of the opinion that more loans might advantageously be made and that the bank should be provided with additional reserves so that it could make them. Suppose, therefore, they purchase $20 million of securities (corporation stock) in the open market. The seller of the securities would deposit in the commercial bank the money he received in payment (the Reserve authorities' cheque). The commercial bank in turn would deposit it in its reserve account at the Reserve Bank. Having these additional reserves of $20 million, the commercial bank, by making loans, could increase its deposits to five times as much, or $100 million — $20 million being the 20 percent reserves required against deposits of $100 million."

Page 71: "The same principle that would hold if there were only one bank holds true of all banks taken together " (All banks must be ONE. — the author.) ... "By the normal and active process of clearing the enormous number of cheques that are constantly being drawn on one bank and deposited in another — thereby entailing the transfer of funds from one reserve balance of one bank to the reserve balance of another."

Page 75: "The practical consequence of this is that the Federal Reserve authorities, by supplying a relatively small volume of additional reserve funds, make it possible for the banking system as a whole to supply the public with a far greater additional volume of credit."

Note bottom Page 75: "The reserves required are not 20 percent at present (1938), but about 15 percent is the average. The figure 20 percent has been used for greater simplicity in illustration." Page 84: "(*The Nature of Federal Reserve Bank Credit.*) Credit in general is a matter of monetary agreement, the essence of it being an acceptable promise to pay. Bank credit is a special form of credit, peculiar in that it involves a promise or assumption of liability by a bank, given in exchange for a promise made to the bank. Thus the bank accepts a promissory note of a customer and in exchange promises to pay the customer a corresponding amount, which, pending his order, is carried on its books as a deposit in his favour.

"Bank credit plays a vitally important part in modern economic life. As a source of bank deposits transferable by cheque, it provides the funds with which the bulk of monetary payments is effected. It is always interchangeable with legal tender money, but for the most part it is not derived from legal tender money, nor does the volume of bank credit bear any ... relationship to the volume of legal tender money. If the volume of loans that banks could make and of deposits they could accept were limited to the volume of currency in existence, bank credit would not have the utility (inexhaustibleness) in our economic system." (Bank would be stymied.)

Page 85: "Reserve Bank credit resembles member bank credit in general, but under the law it has a limited and special use — as a source of member bank reserve funds. It is itself a form of money authorized for special purposes, convertible into other forms of money convertible therefrom, and readily controllable as to amount (This is the genesis of created money-bank deposits.)

"Federal Reserve Bank credit, therefore, as already stated, does not consist of funds that the Reserve authorities 'GET' somewhere in order to lend, but constitutes funds that they are empowered to create. (By writing a cheque against no funds. — the author.) The process of creation is one of giving the promise of the Federal Reserve Bank — in the form of Federal Reserve notes and reserve deposits — in exchange for the promise made by others to the Federal Reserve Banks, the reason for the exchange being that the Federal Reserve Banks' promises are recognized by law as having a particular monetary utility not possessed by the promises of individuals and institutions. That is, Federal Reserve Bank promises — or 'liabilities,' as they are commonly called — serve in the form of Federal Reserve notes as the principal element of the circulating medium..."

Page 94: " A striking feature is the abrupt increase in the gold stock in 1934. This reflects revaluation of the dollar by which the price of gold was raised from $20.67 to $35 an ounce." Page 106: "... the surplus of the Federal Reserve banks is now (1938) about $149,000,000. This, with their capital of about $135 million gives them capital and surplus combined about

$248 million." (It's about $350 billion now.)

That comprises the definite statements of the Reserve Board in 1939, which specifically asserts that when bankers make loans and buy investment obligations they just give the borrowers, and sellers of investment obligations, deposit credits on their books, and the aggregate deposits are increased.

As you read what follows, if a doubt arises in your mind that "what I say can't be true," reread these quotations, for they give you a complete picture of banking under the Federal Reserve System, and you will be convinced that the banking business as a whole is a crime, and should be abolished.

Don't reject what I shall say, unless, after testing what I say by the above quotations, you find I do not I have proof that what I say is true.

CHAPTER III

WHAT THE LEADERS OF MEN

HAVE SAID ABOUT MONEY

In the past those who have tried to change our monetary system, have been "greenbackers," "Free Coinagers," and " 16-to-oners." These reached their highest altitude of absurdities in "Coin" Harvey, who wanted to load the buyer down with tonnages of "Silver Dollars" beyond the power of the transportation system to carry from buyer to seller.

All of them have kept their eyes and their readers' eyes so close to currency (bills and coins) that they could never see either the fallacy of thinking of money in terms of "cash," currency, or of trying to carryon modern business by transporting tons of currency back and forth between buyers and sellers, living in remote points from each other.

But it has been necessary to keep the people believing that cash is the real money of the Nation in order that bankers may continue to hide behind the lie that they are lending the depositors' money. That they have had many columns of deposits, but only a fragment of the total deposits to the credit of all of the people, appears in the only two items mentioned in their "meaningless public statements."

You will find listed "Demand deposits, subject to cheques" and "Time deposits against which no cheque can be drawn." The totals of these two deposit accounts, let me repeat, are miniature in comparison to the total of other accounts, which are hundreds of billions of dollars to the credit of Bankers (the bank), of the rich who have non-chequeing accounts of the saving institutions, of the many lending agencies.

Then there are billions in the forms of investment obligations (United States bonds, Promissory Notes, Mortgages, Deed of Trust, etc.) which may be quickly transmuted into deposit credits, subject to cheques.

And these hundreds of billions of deposits and investment obligations (nascent money) are money, and may be used in the buying of anything of value, services and pleasures. They lie there, for the most part, dormant, ready to emerge from their hibernation to crowd the production dollar, the earned dollar out of the markets. But let's quote some of these men who have talked about money, banking:

Rothschild said:

"Let me have the power to issue and control a Nation's money, and I care not who writes its laws."

He was a top stock market gambler, and loved the game because of its hazards and its easy takes for the ins.

Jack Woodford said:

"As an ex-banker and one who has scuttled quite largely about this country of ours, I give you my solemn word of honour that I have never seen any other class more corrupt, conscienceless, and thieving than bankers."

Congressman Wright Patman said:

"The Government, under the Constitution, has the power to create all the money. It issues both money and bonds, and sells the bonds to the bankers that create deposit money. If banks need the cash to pay the depositors, the Treasury supplies it free. In that way, Congress has farmed out to private bankers the nation's credit free, and Congress' power to create money, the greatest and most profitable privilege our Nation had, absolutely free; and of course, unconstitutionally.

"Congress has farmed out to selfish private banking corporations the credit of the nation free, and empowered them to create all of the people's money. Some day the American people are going to blame this 1943 Congress for not changing the system at this time as we are entering on a $300 billion war program."

Mr. Eccles, then the Chairman of the Reserve Board, said in replying to a question asked him when he was testifying before the Ways and Means Committee of the House, in February 1943: Mr. Patman.

"Mr. Eccles, the $20 billion of United States Bonds the bankers now own — they created at the time they bought the bonds the money that they paid for them did they not?

Mr. Eccles:

"That is the function of a bank. When a bank makes a loan to a utility, or a farmer, it creates the money that it lends at the time the loan is made."

Congressman Voorhis:

"The Government should create money, not lend it; banks should lend money but not create it."

Congressman Callaway:

"I voted against the Federal Reserve Act because it gives the bankers the power of life and death over every person in the nation."

Nicholas Biddle, president of the Second United States Bank: "Andy, I can make or break any business man in the Nation."

Andy Jackson, the intrepid Indian fighter, asked

"And how can you do that Nick?" And Nick replied: "By extending or withholding a loan." And Andy shot back, "Then, Nick, by the eternal I'll kill your bank";— and he did.

And that was exactly what he wanted Andy to do because Nick's heart was set on private banking; and from that calamitous act of Andy in the 1830's, the Nation has lived a hectic life at the mercy of private banks that would organize, issue money far beyond their ability to "redeem," use this money to buy property and pleasures, then bust, leaving the depositors broke. Sir Josiah Stamp, while in Austin in the 20's, in an informal talk to about 150 professors of the University of Texas, said:

"Banking was conceived in iniquity and born in sin... Bankers own the earth. Take it away from them but leave them the power to create money, and, with a flick of the pen, they will create enough money to buy it back again. .. . Take this great power away from them and all great fortunes like mine (he was the second richest man in Great Britain, and president of the Bank of England) will disappear, and they ought to disappear, for then this would be a better and a happier world to live in.... My sons are well educated; they should not hesitate to take their places in the ranks of humanity, and forge their own fortunes... BUT, if you want to continue to be the slaves of bankers and pay the cost of your own slavery, then let bankers continue to create money and control Credit."

Senator Robert L. Owen of Oklahoma in a preface to a book written by Winslow and Brogham, wrote:

"It would appear that there could be no subject of more supreme importance to the people of the United States than an understanding of money and its powers. It is remarkable, and a fact of surpassing importance, that the provision of the Constitution of the United States authorizing Congress exclusively to coin money and regulate the value thereof has been overlooked by American statesmen. Their failure to perceive the deep significance of this language of the Constitution has resulted in the indefensible expansion and contraction of money by private persons, bringing on monetary depressions periodically."

Mr. Owen was chairman of the Senate Banking Committee in 1913, and managed the Federal Reserve Act legislation. It is strange that he, a then "statesman," overlooked the Constitutional provision that said definitely that Congress could not surrender its powers to a private corporation.

President Lincoln, after he had been compelled to give Great Britain control over the finances of the United States in exchange for Great Britain's financing the Civil War, and following the banking act of 1863, said:

"As a result of the Civil War, corporations (Banking) have been enthroned and an era of corruption in high places will follow and the money power of the country will endeavour to prolong its reign by working on the prejudices of the people until wealth is aggregated in the hands of a few, and the republic is destroyed. I feel at this moment more anxiety for the safety of my country than ever before, even in the midst of war."

Bismarck said:

"The death of Lincoln is a disaster for Christendom. I fear that foreign bankers with their craftiness and tortuous tricks will entirely control the exuberant riches of America and use it to corrupt modern civilization. They will not hesitate to plunge the whole world into wars and chaos, in order that they may inherit the earth."

How prophetic. The three world wars, and this cold war; and the present stringency of credit, invoked by the Federal Reserve authorities.

The President of the American Bankers Association, speaking in their convention, in 1931, almost two years after they pulled the stock market down into one of its worst crashes said:

"We the men in this hall, who control the economic destiny of the Nation, knew in 1927 that this terrible depression was coming, and we did nothing about it."

Of course they did nothing about it. They planned it, and carried it to a successful (for them) conclusion.

And he could have quoted the American Bankers Association as having said, in 1891:

"We authorize you (our loan agents in the western states) to loan funds on good real estate to fall due not later than September 1, 1894, and at no time thereafter. And on and after that date we will not renew our loans under any consideration. But on September 1, 1894, we will demand our money. We will foreclose and become Mortgagees in possession. We can in this way take two-thirds of the farms west of the Mississippi and thousands of them east of the Mississippi as well, at our own price. We will own three-fourths of the farms of the West and the money of the nation. Then farmers will become tenants as in England."

Comment: Thus they planned panics of 1893, and reaped harvests of farms in 1894, as planned in 1891. In fact every panic, "depression," and the present threatened "recession," which will be in the language of a Dallas banker, "A honey," was blueprinted and managed by the bankers of America directed by the bankers of London, Berlin, Paris.

The American Bankers Association, one week after Grover Cleveland was inaugurated, on March 11, 1893, sent the following letter to all bankers:

"Dear Sir: The interest of National Banks requires immediate financial legislation by Congress. Silver, silver certificates and U.S. Treasury notes must be retired.

National Bank Notes on a gold basis must be made the only money. This will require the authorization of $500 million to $1 billion new U.S. Bonds as basis of circulation. You will — MUST retire at once one-third of your circulation, and call in loans. (They got this in 1934! They never quit.)

"Be careful to make a monetary stringency among your patrons, especially among influential business men. Advocate extra session of Congress to repeal the silver purchasing clause of the Sherman Law. Act with other banks of your city in securing a large petition to Congress for its repeal. Use personal influence with your Congressmen, and particularly let your wishes be known to your Senators.

The future of National Banks, as fixed and safe investments, depends on immediate action, as there is an increasing sentiment in favour of Government legal tender notes-bills and silver."

Ex-President John Adams wrote to his friend Ex-President Thomas Jefferson, and said:

"All the perplexities, confusion and distress in America arise not from defects in our Constitution: not from want of honour or virtue, so much as from downright ignorance of the nature of coin, credit and circulation."

Siegfried said:

"Finance, money, credit, International Banking knows no boundaries of nations, no tongue, no colour, no creed. It is the universal language of *exploitation and tyranny.* It robs the American farmer, the Welch miner, the Czech glass workers the toiling, serving and producing men, women and children, with equal complacency. It knows no mastery but its own, no service but to itself, no means but money: it will brook no opposition."

John Skelton Williams, Comptroller of the Currency, said to the Deflation Committee of the American Bankers Association, in 1920, in protest of their resolution to contract money and credit (exactly what bankers of 1957 are doing):

"Don't you know that this will break every little bank in the country?"

And the bankers replied cold-bloodedly: "They ought to break; there are too many of them." But, he retorted:

"Don't you know that it is going to ruin lots of farmers?" Again they replied cold-bloodedly:

"They ought to be ruined; they are getting so prosperous (following World War I) they won't work."

You only have to recall the late 20's and 30's to remember how thoroughly the bankers busted the little banks, the farmers, and the small business men.

Henry Ford said:

"Here is a nation that might be the richest nation on earth, when actually we haven't enough of anything, because there is not enough production. The need is here. The ability to produce is here. The people are eager to produce — willing to work. The stoppage is the system that puts profits before production — and that is the money system."

A final personal story: A local linotype operator in Austin, who is steadily employed, got a notice from a local finance company (and all of them are children of bankers, through whom they shunt their mountains of deposit credits in their surplus and undivided profits columns) informing him that he had a $400 loan without investigation or bother, for him, if he would come in and claim it. Well, the working man's family never have their wants satisfied; so he went down and was met with glad hands and unction dripped from the lender's jowls.

Without "investigation" for the lender had done that, finding the man regularly employed, a loan agreement (not a note) was laid before him, for his signature, with the assurance that he (the lender) would complete all the papers, and send them to him in a few days. The man couldn't suspect such a nice man's being tricky; so he signed the loan agreement, for that is what it amounted to, and the lender handed him a cheque, and wished his victim on his way. Said the borrower to me: "In a few days I got the papers and found that my life had been insured, the debt had been insured, and costs of making the loan had been added; and instead of my loan agreement calling for my payment in instalments of $400 and interest, it called for a total payment of $676 in instalments," and that loan agency is a department of an Austin bank. And my final quote from our Constitution:

Article 1. Section 1: All legislative power herein granted shall be vested in a Congress of the United States, which shall consist of a Senate and a House of Representatives.

Section 8: The Congress shall have power ... to coin money, regulate the value thereof, and of foreign coin, and fix the standard of weights and measures.

Section 10: No state shall ... coin money, emit bills of credit, make anything but gold and silver coin tender in payment of debt "

Then, Constitutionally, there could be no state bank chartered. Congressman Wright Patman has said:

"The Government of the United States, under the Constitution, has the power, and it is the duty of the Government, to CREATE ALL MONEY... This being true, why should Congress sit idly by and allow the (private) banks to expand $20 to $1, or even $50 to $1, in order to finance the war and the other costs of Government when it is nothing more nor less than Congress permitting the credit of this Nation to be farmed out for the selfish benefit of private banking corporations? The Treasury issues both money and bonds. Under the present system it sells (deposits) the bonds to a (the) bank(s) that creates money (bank deposits)! Then, if the bank needs the actual money, the actual printed greenbacks (or coins) to pay the depositors, the Treasury will furnish that money to pay the depositors. In that way Congress farms out the use of the government's (nation's) credit absolutely free.

"It is the duty of Congress to issue — coin or create-money and regulate its value under the Constitution. This great privilege has been farmed out free to the privately owned banks by Congress. This privilege is worth billions of dollars a year to those exercising it under laws passed by Congress.

"The United States Treasury prints and issues both the interest-bearing bonds and the money (bills and coins) which is another form of Government obligation, not interest-bearing.

"The Reserve banks are owned by the private commercial banks, including the bank that bought the bonds. The Federal Reserve banks are Federal in name only; they are owned lock, stock and barrel by the private commercial banks, which have invested a very small sum of money upon which they get 6% per annum.

"Remember, the U.S. Treasury has caused the Bureau of Engraving and Printing to print and deliver to the Federal Reserve Bank a million dollars in U.S. Government bonds, interest bearing, and then it added a million dollars in currency. Each is a Government obligation. The Federal Reserve Bank delivers to the local commercial bank the million dollars in bonds and obtains for the Government a million dollars in bank deposits which it cheques out to pay its debts. Then the Reserve Bank delivers to the local commercial bank the million dollars in cash.

"The present banking system, thru the use of the Government's credit, as now (1943) proposed to finance the war can issue more than $240 billions in money, and every bit of it will be issued on the banks' $8 billions capital and surplus and the Government's credit. Of course, it will be the Government's credit that will make it secure, as the $8 billions will be insufficient for that purpose... The Government pays interest for the use of its own credit.

"Who created such a system that is costing the taxpayers $1,750,000,000 this year (1942) and will cost the taxpayer $4,500,000,000 a year (years and years ahead) when our anticipated expenditures for [our] war purposes are made? The answer is that such a system was built up over a long period of years (from 1781 to 1942). Congress (has) passed monetary laws without giving a great deal of attention to them, being told (by bankers who had written the bills) that money was (is) a mystery and that few people understood it and those understanding it were the ones wanting the laws. It was (and is) smart (alecky) for a Congressman to say, 'All I know about money is that I don't have enough of it,' or some similar crack that invariably drew laughter and applause, and the bill was passed (practically as the bankers wrote it). If some person who had given the subject thought and consideration attempted to show how the credit of the Nation was being farmed out FREE to privately owned commercial banks, he could be silenced very quickly by a whispering campaign that he was a monetary crackpot, or a greenbacker, who wanted to flood the country with worthless printing-press money. Then, with a few references to continental currency, fiat money, and German inflation, the bill was sent on its way. All such bills were referred to as a bill to further strengthen our sound currency.

"I am opposed to the Government, which has the sovereign and exclusive power to create money, paying private bankers for the use of its own money. The private bankers do not lend their money to the Government; they lend the Government's money to the Government, and collect interest annually. I want to say that the highest authority and best in our Government, the President of the Federal Reserve System, the Secretary of the Treasury, as well as all informed people, admit it.

The banks say they lend the depositors' money; 'we're responsible for it, and if we don't get any interest for its use, we just won't buy any bonds.' But they know that is not so for the President of the Federal Reserve System, Mr. Eccles said, 'We create credit to buy bonds. That is all we have ever done. That is the way the Federal Reserve System operates. It creates money.' The Secretary of the Treasury, Mr. Morgenthau said:

'When commercial banks buy bonds they do not pay for them with real cash taken from their vaults (nor out of their capital or surplus - out of no existing funds), but by placing on their books newly created bank deposits to the credit of the Government.' "

I was reluctant to admit that the wrongs I found in the West bank were universally practiced; yet I had heard all of my life of banks closing their doors, and the depositors losing all; then came the deluge in 1933, just 20 years after the passage of the Federal Reserve Act, when every bank in the United States closed; and while the depositors did not lose all, millions were lost to them.

Charley Dawes, ex-vice-president of the United States, and at the time head of the Reconstruction Finance Corporation, hung to his post until he was granted a $90 million Refinance loan to resurrect his Chicago Bank.

Then is when Congress should have said to the banking boys: "We gave you every law for 100 years that you wrote and asked us to pass. Finally in 1913 we gave you the Federal Reserve Act, on your assuring us sound money, panic-free banking methods, and top to bottom prosperity for the people of the United States would follow. But here you come up after a 20- year trial under this act, ask the President by Executive Order to close all banks for re-organization and "getting-our-breath" again.

"We shall return the creation of money to the hands of Congress where the Constitution reposed it; and take over the mechanics of money (keeping of the depositors' accounts, cashing and clearing their cheques), and return you boys to the actualities of money lending: you will lend only the money you have to 'the credit of yourselves on the books of the United States Depositories, which we shall scatter over the United States as prodigally as post offices."

After all this had taken place, and I had been crying for years that all banking laws are unconstitutional because the Founding Fathers said specifically:

Article I, Section 8: (Sixth Power) "The Congress shall have power ... To coin money, regulate the value thereof, and of foreign coin, and fix the standard of weights and measures.

And in Section 10: "No state shall enter into any treaty, alliance, or confederation, grant letters of marque and reprisal ; coin money; emit bills of credit; make anything but gold and silver coin a tender in payment of debts..." Therefore, no state or private banks.

I want to prove to you with facts and figures., and documentary evidence, that our banking system is wholly wrong, unconstitutional, and wholly bad; then I want you to understand that bankers, in order that they might continue to profit through their power to create money and control credit, have been doing three indispensable public services: (1) creating money, (2) keeping the depositors' accounts, and cashing and clearing their cheques, and (3) lending money. The first two are Constitutional functions of Congress, the third is a private property right.

Return to the Congress the "coining of money," and its control that it may regulate the value of money, and add the mechanics of money as developed by the Reserve System, and we will have the safest, soundest, most elastic and fluid money the world has ever known.

Then you have no bank failures, for there will be no banks — there will be only U.S. Treasury Depositories; and bankers will then become just money lenders, not money creators.

CHAPTER IV

THE LEGALIZED CRIME OF BANKING

I reprint the first 11 pages of a 16-page pamphlet printed July 4, 1951. It is the full story of the creation of money by the Reserve Banks, with all of the camouflage torn away. The enormity of the crime of banking strikes you a stunning blow when you read that the bankers profited in the last World War over a trillion dollars, and the people lost that amount, plus the lives of many of our manhood's best, and billions in property destruction. Read this story as a starter of that completer story to follow.

Facts About Banking
Every Citizen Should Know

When you tear away from money the many confusing false statements bankers have used to camouflage, to obscure their corrupt and thieving practices, you will find that money is not a mysterious thing. They have kept men's minds confused, knowing it is in confusion that they are safest from the discovery of their crimes.

They drilled into our minds that only a fool will try to understand money so well that even their victims and slaves hurl at one who tries to explain money to them, "He's a nut; gone crazy on money," and they flee from the man who would liberate them! Aye more! They will hold the bankers' coats while the latter crucify him!

Let's remove the camouflage and expose not only the crimes of banking, but the simplicity of money

1. The Government *does not create* nor issue money. Banks *create* and issue all our money

2. Coins and currency are not money-just tokens. Our money is bank credit in the form of bank deposits.

3. Banks do not lend cash, currency-coins or bills. They do not lend their own capital, surplus or profits. Not their depositors' deposits; nor their own credit; nor the nation's credit. *Period.* Bankers do not lend money or anything; they only buy notes (your note), mortgages, bonds, securities, money, or other investment obligations; and they pay for them with bank credit in the form of *new bank deposits* which they *create* at the time they make the purchase.

In a hearing in Congress, in February, 1943, Cong. Wright Patman asked Marriner S. Eccles., Chairman of the Board of Governors of the Federal Reserve System, "... the U.S. Bonds ($20,000,000,000) the banks hold today - they *created* the money to buy those bonds, did they not?" And Mr. Eccles replied, "The banking system as a whole *creates* the (bank) *deposits* as (at the time) they make loans and investments, whether they buy Government bonds, or whether they buy utility bonds, or whether they make farmers' loans.."

4. Strictly speaking the term "Bank Deposits" is erroneous You have "Bank Credits," and they were *created* by the banks at the time they bought your note or any other investment obligation. Nothing was deposited, therefore there could not be bank deposits.

5. You do not have cash, coins and bills, on deposit. You own only the cash in your possession. You bought it from the bank, paying for it with bank credits to your account. You do not deposit cash in the bank. You sell the cash back to the bank, and it pays for it with *new* bank credits.

Quoting from the booklet, "The Federal Reserve System - Its Purposes and Functions," published in May, 1939, by the Board of Governors of the Federal Reserve System; "Treasury currency ... is placed in circulation through Federal Reserve Banks, the Banks giving the Treasury credit in its chequeing account for the amount. The Reserve Banks keep a large stock of cash on hand, principally Federal Reserve notes which are their own (private corporation) liabilities, printed by the Government at the expense of Reserve Banks (30c per $1,000). There are two principal ways by which any individual gets bills and coins. Either he draws it out of his bank and has it charged to his account *(buys* it); or he is paid for his labour, his services, or his goods with money that has been drawn out of a bank (bought) by some one."

6. There is no gold standard. There never was. All of it was a hoax. We have no standard, measure of the value of money, the dollar. It is a private corporation dollar with no substance of value behind it. It is just a bank credit transferable by cheque wherewith customers of banks make the great bulk of their monetary payments. Its value as with spuds is based on supply "on the market." Cheap money as with cheap spuds indicates glutted market.

7. The terms Bank Reserves, Bank Credits, Re-discount, etc., are fictitious ponies bankers stable as ringers. They are figments of bankers' imagination, 'funds' that banks are empowered to create. The act of creation is one giving the promises of banks in exchange for your note or some other investment obligation. See page 85 of the Reserve booklet.

8. Proof that all you know about money and banking is false is found on pages 39- 40 of Reserve booklet:

"The aggregate deposits in the banking system as a whole represent mainly funds lent by banks or paid by banks for notes, mortgages, and other forms of investment obligations. It may seem that it should be the other way round - that bank loans and investments would be derived from bank deposits instead of bank deposits being derived from loans and investments (well, bankers have told you that they loan their depositors' deposits, haven't they?); and it is true that deposits would not grow out of loans (and investments) if currency were to be used by the public for monetary payments to the exclusion of bank deposits transferable by cheque. But as it is, the public in general prefers to have its monetary funds, including what it borrows, on deposit in banks rather than in the form of currency in its own possession. The result of this preference is that the proceeds of loans (and investments) go on deposit to be disbursed by cheque, and aggregate deposits are increased... a bank's purchase of investments, i.e., notes, mortgages, bonds, etc., is an extension of credit just as loans do."

On page 55: "Loans and purchases of securities by the Federal Reserve authorities are one of the important sources of member bank reserves; member bank reserves in turn are the basis of member bank credit; that is, of the loans and investments of member banks. And member bank credit is a source of the bank deposits transferable by cheque wherewith business men and other persons make the bulk of their monetary payments."

On page 56: "The reserves which member banks are required to maintain are only a fraction of their deposits (ranging from *5%* to *25%*). Suppose banks were required to maintain *20%* and that they had *20%* and no more. Then if their deposits were to be increased by $500,000,000, they would have to have their reserves increased by $100,000,000. Accordingly, $100,000,000 of Federal Reserve bank credit obtained by the purchase of securities by the Federal Reserve authorities would increase their reserves sufficiently to enable the banks to expand their own credit by $500,000,000," and this would enable them to make loans and buy securities to the amount of $500,000,000, which would increase the bank deposits $500,000,000."

On page 85: "Federal Reserve Bank credit, under the law, has a limited and special use-as a source of member bank reserve funds. It is itself a form of money. It does not consist of funds the Reserve authorities GET somewhere in order to lend, but constitutes funds that they are empowered to CREATE." To create is to bring substance out of a void, out of nothingness.

The Creative Acts of Banks

Quoting from same Reserve booklet, page 70, the creative steps are given in succinct form: "Suppose that the Reserve authorities were of the opinion that more loans might advantageously (to bankers) be made and the bank should be provided with additional reserves so that it could make them. Suppose they purchased $20,000,000 of securities (corporation stock) in the open market. The sellers of the stock would deposit in the commercial bank the $20 million cheque (drawn against no deposits - Reserve authorities created $20 million by writing the cheque) they receive in payment. The commercial bank in turn would deposit the cheque in its reserve account at its Reserve Bank. Having the $20,000,000 additional reserves, the commercial bank, by making loans (or buying securities), could increase its deposits to five times as much, or $100,000,000 the $20 million being the 20% reserves required against the $100 million of new deposits."

Analysing this story we find there are five steps in the process of creating bank deposits:

1.   Reserve authorities buy corporation securities or Government Bonds, giving to the corporation a cheque against no funds in payment.

2.   The corporation deposits the cheque in its home bank, creating new bank deposits.

3.   The bank re-deposits it in its Reserve Bank, creating *new* bank reserves which are credited to its reserve account on the Reserve Bank's books.

4. The commercial bank enters on its books as bank credit a sum five times its reserves on Reserve books.

5. The bank creates the $100 million *new* bank deposits by making loans to its customers or by buying investment obligations, in above example.

Summarizing, we reveal these astounding figures:

Corporation securities offering 6%	$20 million
Reserve cheque in payment.	$20 million
New bank deposits to corporation.	$20 million
New bank reserves, credit of bank.	$20 million
New bank credits on its books.	$100 million
New bank deposits to cr. of cust.	$100 million
New active monetary values.	$140 million

In the process the banks created $120 million bank deposits, came into ownership of the $20 million corporation stock and $100 million in personal notes, mortgages, bonds etc. They will re-sell the corporation stock and add the $20 million bank deposits they receive for them to their profit account, for the stock did not cost them a thin dime. In due course of time the bankers get bank deposits for all loans and will re-sell all securities, and add this $100 million plus interest to their account, making a total of $120 million plus interest and dividends the bankers add to their profit accounts when the cycle is completed.

The $20 million Reserve cheque, the $20 million corporation stock, $20 million bank reserves, the $100 million bank credit—none of it cost the bankers one thin dime; therefore the $100 million in notes, mortgages, etc., which they bought with the bank credit cost them not one thin dime. Then the $120 million profit they added to their account cost them not one thin dime.

Their customers got the use of the $100 million at heavy interest cost, for just a short time, then it became the permanent assets of the bankers. The whole process was just simple bookkeeping. *That's how Sir Josiah Stamp meant bankers would with the flick of a pen create enough money to buy the world back again!"*

Legalized Robbery

The United States Government issued more than $250 billion U.S. bonds during World War II.

The Federal Reserve Banking System bought every bond, giving the Government deposit credit on the books of the Reserve Banks. The Federal Reserve Banking System is a 100% private corporation, "federal" in name only.

Let's summarize the magic touch of bankers. The Treasury wrote cheques totalling $250 billion. The recipients deposited these cheques in commercial banks, creating $250 billion deposits to the credit of those who served the Nation, or sold the United States goods. Banks sent them to Reserve Banks, increasing their reserves $250 billion. Then the banks wrote on their books $1.25 trillion additional bank credits, which they could lend or use to buy securities, which would add $1.25 trillion in new bank deposits. These cheques of the Government first created $250 billion deposits then created $250 billion bank reserves, which ballooned into

$1,250 billion Bank Credit!

In due time the commercial banks will collect all loans and re-sell all securities. This will transfer from their customers' deposit accounts $1.25 trillion to the banks' profit account. Now let's total up banks' war profits:

U.S. Bonds	*$250,000,000,000*
Deposits to banks' accounts.	*1,250,000,000,000*
The price-of-the World-War-II total.	*$1,500,000,000,000*

Adding the $250 billion deposits that the banks paid the Government for the bonds and we find the war created $1,750,000,000,000 monetary assets, and only the $250 billion the Reserve Banks paid the Government escape their assets, but they have the U.S. Bonds, which cost them not one thin dime.

And they sell the U.S. Bonds daily which will finally transfer the $250 billion deposits they gave for the Bonds - and the complete ownership will be theirs!

There Sir Josiah was vindicated in one war. With a flick of fountain pens the bankers created, in five years, $1.75 trillion in monetary values! and at the end of the cycle securities and deposits are their assets. And none of it cost the bankers one thin dime.

They are mad men madly plunging the World into World War III - Creditalism's Armageddon. The people pay for the wars in materials, human sacrifice - the cold corpses and mangled living bodies of their sons, in anguish, toil, sweat, tears and blood yet they plod back to empty larder in a roofless home, and before they can eat or buy material to build their home and a lot to rest it on, they must fall upon their knees before these bankers, who contributed no materials, no sweat, few tears and little blood: who *made $1.75 trillion just by selling Uncle Sam the Nation's own credit, for enough of these $1.75 trillion of bank credit to build their little cottages. With cold indifference the bankers said, "You have no credit. You must get the Government to indorse your notes." That to the men who had fought, while these bankers stole from them and the rest of us (legally) $250 billion in U.S. bonds and $1.25 trillion in bank credit.*

Beef steaks selling at $1.1 a pound, $30 land selling for $400, a $1234 cottage selling for $5275, is the result of this increase of bank deposits, inflation of money. High prices are not inflation:

they grow out of the inflation of money. Price rises should keep pace with money increases. The Government's price controls is an effort, in obedience to the orders of the Reserve Banks, to compel the people to accept, for their goods and services, a cheap dollar. Only the deposits in chequeing accounts reflect the money supply. That's why bankers, aided and abetted by the Government, beat down wages, then take every pay day huge sums as taxes; fight for higher utility profits; urge you to put your money into savings accounts, and urge you to purchase U.S. Bonds and corporation securities. A hungry house wife drools as she sees the thick juicy $1.1 steak, touches it shyly, and lifts a soup bone into the shiny grocery cart, and hurries away. If all deposit dollars were demand deposits, and there were no price controls, steaks would cost $11 a pound and $300 salary would be $3,000 a month!

The worthless German mark would be worth more! Why the difference? The German marks, were printed, in the hands of the people; the American dollars are figures on bankers' ledgers. The American bankers are set to follow Germany's lead. Rumnl has said, "Banks will not bust as in the 30's; as often as the depositors ask for cash, greenbacks will be handed out to them." These will be Federal Reserve notes, which cost them only 30c per

$1,000, and they will pay Uncle Sam the thirty cents with new deposit dollars, which cost the bankers not one thin dime. The greenbacks you get will be fiat money, redeemable in its kind, like giving a hot cheque for a hot cheque! Look at a Federal Reserve note. Read, ""Redeemable in Lawful Money." Not in silver, Not in gold. It is lawful Money. "On demand" the banker or Treasury of the United States, would hand you another Reserve [corporation fiat] note. But the Government has already printed for the Reserve Banks $21,964,687,524 (May 31, 1957 circulation statement of United States Money), Federal Reserve Gold Certificates, not for circulation, which bankers hold. This gives them title to our entire gold. It cost them just to have them engraved $8 million. And they paid this with new hot deposits. In this way bankers got title to $21,964,687,524 (billion) of gold absolutely free!

Congressman Wright Patman said before, the Ways and Means Committee of the House, February 13, 1943:

"I am opposed to the U.S. Government, which has the sovereign and exclusive power of creating money, paying private bankers for the use of its money. The private banking corporations do not hire their own money to the Government; they hire only the Government's money, credit, to the Government, and collect an interest annually."

It is now approximately $10 billion annually. They got $250 billion U.S. Bonds gratis. The people must pay the bonds, too!

Congressman Jerry Voorhis said:

"Banks should lend money, not create it. The Government should create money, but not lend it." The Constitution says:

"The Congress shall have the power to coin money, regulate the value thereof."

But it nowhere empowers Congress to re-delegate this power to private corporations.

There is a solution of this problem. It requires no revolutionary change - just a change of control and of management. The present system is dangerous. Utterly fails to give us a sound stable money. Invites wild speculation and ill-advised and wasteful investments. Corporations water their stock as much as 168 times their physical values (See the Borah Committee Report). It is unconstitutional. Our proposed change is just following the simple, plain mandate of the Constitution, eliminating the wrongs of banking, and giving us a sound,

non-fluctuating-in-buying-power-and-volume dollar. It does no man a wrong. It gives no man an unfair advantage over another, no man a special privilege. It stimulates legitimate businesses, places a premium on honest labour and industry, protects the weak against the strong, and cuts the shackles of economic bondage from the masses and saves them from trillions in debt and billions in interest payments. It is Constitutional Admittedly so.

Had we made change in 1933, and the Treasury had taken credit for $250 billion, we would not owe the $279,764,369,348 (as of February 28, 1956) bonds with the $10 billion annual interest payments. Banks would not hold gratis $1,750 billion in bank credit. We would have just the $279 billion new, and excess deposits which the $10 billion interest we now pay would cancel out in 25 years. As it is, we'll pay in interest the $279 billion and still owe the banks the $279 billion in bonds, along with the $1,750 billion they got in addition to the bonds.

The banks render two essential services: 1. lending credit, or money; 2. keeping deposits, clearing and cashing cheques. The first is a private property right and should be reserved to the people; the second is a public right and must be reserved to the Nation.

The system of keeping the people's money credits, cashing and clearing their cheques, if divorced from the lending of money, would give us the best medium of exchange, money, the world has ever devised. And, if the Nation carefully limits its volume to the amount needed to carry on the business of the Nation on an annual basis, it will be the most fluid and the soundest money on earth.

(Note: Perhaps I should explain why I used different figures in different summations of the costs of World War II. I did it that I might play with the $250 billion, and the official $276 billion. I used the 20% figures as the percentage of deposits to reserves, as the Reserve Book did, but would have been closer to the 'truth had I used the ratio of 7 instead of 5; and now the Reserve Banks are asking Congress to let them loan 10 times their reserves. Of course that would have doubled all of my totals, if I had used 10 instead of five. The alarming fact, and not the exact figures, was my object always. - The Author.)

CHAPTER V

BANKERS WANT DOUBLE OR NOTHING

Well, Josiah Stamp said that so long as a nation will let private corporations create money and control credit, one is foolish not to be a banker. Too, you have heard that there is no better way to learn than by doing. So let's you and I go into the banking business. I don't mean that we shall buy stocks in some bank. We are going to be top dogs or nothing - in this our make- believe story.

There is a little story behind this, decision. We have been trying for years to get a bank on the wrong side of the river. The big uptown banks blocked us year after year because they didn't quite own the earth, and didn't want opposition, I believe it is called competition. Since the big boys control our Banking Commission, the commission sat and patiently listened to our plea for a bank charter, and would always say no. But you and I finally got the charter, and scraped up $200,000, with another $100,000 for surplus, and were soon in the banking business, and I mean *the banking business* in a big way.

When we got our charter, we went to Washington and bought from the Reserve Bank $200,000 U.S. Bonds. Let me add that we organized a South Austin National Bank, which gave us front seat on this master stock exchange. Well that was good business for we had "invested our capital" in the best securities on earth, the promise of Uncle Sam to pay, U.S. Bonds, so it was not long until we were clipping coupons, and handing them over to Uncle Sammy, and he was handing us cash. Within a year we had collected $7,000, but that is chicken feed in our language.

Well, you neophytes are wondering where we are going to get any money to lend. We have already lent our capital to Uncle Sam! Uncle Sam is the nicest old fellow you ever saw. When we got the bonds, he smiled and said, "Sonnies, just to show you how much I appreciate my enterprising boys, take this $200,000 in cash just as a present." Now, what do you know about that? We go to Washington with a cheque book, write a cheque to the Reserve Bank for $200,000, and get for that cheque against just ordinary bank deposits we had piled up in Austin, $200,000 in U.S. Bonds, and $200,000 in cash. That certainly doubled our money before we got our doors open to lend our neighbours money. (Note: We used Uncle Sammy instead of the Reserve Bank, because in reality Uncle Sam stands behind them, and is endorser of all that they do.)

Well, you look at me and I look at you and both of us are wondering how we are going to keep robbers off our trail as we return to Texas with all of that $200,000 in cash. Uncle Sam, seeing our perplexed expressions, said, "Now, boys, you will not need all that cash to do business on. Since you are a country bank (he knew we were on the wrong side of the river) you will need only $32,000 in the vault just leave all of the cash here in your reserve fund. The Reserve Bank will send you the $32,000 cash when you build your vault and get ready for business, and the $168,000 will be your reserve fund.

So we came back to Austin, and having spent our last dollar buying U.S. Bonds, we had to find a house we could rent to do banking business in. We could not build.

Finally we found a fellow who agreed to build us a bank building, just a modest one-story structure, with picture window that lets us look out over rolling bare hills except there were scattering live oaks here and there. It sort of hurt our feelings to be put way out of business section, and behind a new trade centre at that, and on a side street but it didn't matter: we now had that better mouse trap.

But finally we moved in, the Reserve Bank sent us the $32,000 to do business on, leaving us the $168,000 in our reserve funds the San Antonio Reserve Bank. Our South Austin friends came in and left deposits with us, even Houston and citizens from other towns came in and left deposits. They wanted to pep us up, you see and that first night our clean, new deposit books shewed that we had on deposit to the credit of our friends $32,000. Well, when we took those deposits we only promised the depositors that we would cash their cheques with cash that cost us nothing or see that they cleared through other banks.

Of course not one in a thousand of our friends knew that when we sent those cheques to our San Antonio Reserve Bank for clearing that it would give us credit for these cheques in our reserve fund, dollar for dollar, which amounted to $32,000. There you are again. Our customers' cheques in our hands doubled: they got $32,000 to their credit on our deposit books, and we got $32,000 to our credit on the Reserve Bank's books. We could have asked the Reserve Bank to send us the whole amount, $32,000 in cash, but not needing the cash, we just left it in our Reserve fund, which raised it to $200,000.

Are you getting dizzy, Sam? Well, let's stop and sort of check up, and shake our heads, and clarify this thing in our minds. We have been used to making *[begin page 55]* pretty big money at 10 to 50 percent on goods we have been selling for thirty years; but never anything like this ever happened to us before. Here are the figures:

Assets

We own U.S. Bonds.	$200,000
We have cash in vault.	$32,000
We have Bank Reserves.	$200,000
Total.	$432,000

Liabilities

Demand Deposits.	$32,000
Net Assets.	$400,000

Of course we have overlooked the $100,000 surplus, but that would just confuse us a little, and it does not amount to much anyway; so we will just let it alone.

But that looks pretty good for first day's business doesn't it, Sam? We went to Washington with a Cashier's cheque for $200,000, and on first day of business we find that our net assets are $400,000. But, Sam, you have not heard or seen anything yet. Tomorrow we will begin lending to Tom, Dick and Harry. We will not lend any of the $32,000 cash we have. We will not lend any of the $200,000 capital we have; (of course our capital is just figures on our books!) nor any of the $100,000 surplus. We will begin lending against that $200,000 reserve fund we have on the Reserve Bank books in San Antonio. We can lend $168,000 of the $200,000. We can lend seven times that amount. So we will just write on our books to our credit seven times $168,000, which swells our lending funds (now called bank credit) to $1,176,000.

Gosh, Sam, here we are millionaires before we lend a dime. And that whole $1,176,000 was gratis money given us just because we are bankers. Uncle Sam gave us the first $200,000 in appreciation of our buying some of his old bonds. Then when our friends came along and deposited their money with us, the Reserve Bank showed its appreciation of us by adding that $32,000 to our reserve fund, which offset the $32,000 we drew out to use in cashing our customers' cheques.

Now that bank credit, total $1,176,000, is as much cash, money to us, Sam, as are those $32,000 deposits to our customers. For we can lend it, use it to buy investment obligations, and should we lend the whole amount, we would have in our vaults, notes, deeds, mortgages, and other good as gold papers totalling $1,176,000! And we can lend it this year, for people are hungry for money.

Now, Sam, it does me good to look at those figures. So let's write them down again.

We own U.S. Bonds. $200,000 We have cash in the vaults 32,000 We have notes, etc. 1,176,000 "Ain't it a grand total. $1,408,000?

Say, Sam, why did we fool away the best part of our lives selling hams and harness? Well, I don't know, Tom. You know that bankers never told us anything about what a nice thing they have, I guess is the reason. We just didn't know this sort of thing could be done.

Yes, replied Tom; but, Sam, I find that we can get more bank credits, if we will just ask for them. I understand that the Reserve authorities will buy corporation stock, and pay for it with a cheque against no funds. Our school bus factory here in South Austin is growing so fast that they are in great need of additional capital.

[begin page 57]

Let's show them how easy it is to issue stock, and sell the stock to the Reserve authorities.

So Tom calls the President of the School Bus Factory and says, "Henry, you were talking to me the other day about your; need of a $1,000,000 for expansion and improvement. I have figured out a way to get the money. Come over and let's talk about it." Henry hurries over, for dangling a $1,000,000 before a hungry corporation president's eyes renews his youth. It is agreed that the Bus Company would print up a $1,000,000 new stock for the corporation. Steck does a beautiful job. And Tom and Henry (I'm Tom, don't forget) hurry by plane to Washington. Trains are too slow now for us Big business men.

We lay the proposition before the Reserve authorities. They agree that in a fast growing city like Austin, an up-and-coming School Bus Factory is entitled to additional capital. So the Reserve authorities buy the $1,000,000 stock in our school Bus Factory, and hand the President of the factory a cheque for $1,000,000. We hurry back; to Austin. Henry deposits the cheque in our bank, and he has $1,000,000 to spend on improvements and extensions and riotous living, too... and all such folks do. My cash chops, were drooling all the time, because I knew that when that cheque cleared through the San Antonio Reserve Bank, those nice boys would not forget to add $1,000,000 to our reserve account, and that I could say to the Reserve Bank, just send me $1,000,000 in cash, and get it; but I left it there, and on a scratch pad I deducted $160,000, leaving us $840,000 to lend. I multiplied that $840,000 by seven, and found that now we could continue to lend money, for it showed that our new bank credit growing out of the fact that the bus company deposited $1,000,000 with us had been increased to $5,880,000!

Of course other banks were hogging in our gold mine, for each time a customer sent a cheque to a person who did business with another bank, when that cheque cleared through the Reserve Banks, I lost from my reserve fund the face of the cheque; but I largely offset that by being such a good fellow in the Country Clubs (Oh, yes, I joined at once on becoming a bank President) and on the golf courses, and at night clubs that many folks would send cheques from other banks for deposit in our bank. And, in a way, that just about evens things up.

Well, it is time to quote that biggest of all bankers, who said in the late 20's:

"Banking was conceived in iniquity and born in sin. ...The bankers own the earth... take it away from them, but leave them in control of credit and the creation of money, and with a flick of the pen they will create enough money to buy it back again... Take this power away from them, and all great fortunes like mine will disappear, and they ought to disappear, for this would then be a better and a happier world to live in... But, if you want to remain the slaves of bankers, and pay the cost of your OWN slavery, let them continue to coin money and control credit... However so long as a nation will permit men to do this, one is foolish to work for a living."

Now, Sam, let's do a little figuring to see what we will be worth ten years from now:

We have upped our capital to.	$750,000
Our surplus is now	$375,000
We have in U.S. Bonds	$750,000
We have collected in interest on bonds.	$105,000
We have collected in interest on notes to borrowers.	$895,000
We have collected notes	7,105,000
We have outstanding notes.	9,372,989
Assets total.	$19,352,989

Our customers' deposits are $6,479,643 ... And, Sam, this is just cash items we are listing... there are those ranches we have bought, that ten acres we bought is now oil... Now, Sam, that we have got the touch of Midas ... oh for the years of old Methuselah - but, Sam, even his 969 years would lack another 969 years making my years long enough. But, Sam, I fear them Damn

Rooshuns are going to come over here and take this golden goose away from us; drat' em!

But, old Bob Thornton of Dallas hasn't beat us much. Give us another 20 years, and we will have over $184,000,000 in assets - oh, damn, Sam, there is that damned ulcer at it again, and I (but surely this is not me?) grab my expansive paunch with my Midas hands, and a grimace contorts my Croesus face!

What a finale!

CHAPTER VI

MONEY — OUR GREATEST PROBLEM

B eing convinced that the greatest problem before the people of the United States is money, its correct functioning, I shall undertake to give you a picture of money as it now functions, and then suggest a remedy. The entire discussion shall be from the standpoint of a depositor- borrower, and I shall seek to make it a story that the man on the street may understand.

No organic body can survive, or remain in a healthy state, unless its bloodstream is filled with pure blood, bearing in its liquid stream the proper food elements, and in the proper proportions. Its tissues starve without the proper amount of food supplied constantly. Whether the body is active, or in a passive state of complete relaxation and rest, the bloodstream must never stop for a moment.

Civilization is an organic body, composed of millions of cells (each a human being), just as the body of a man is composed of millions of cells. Just as the cells of the human body are held together by a centripetal energy, the law of cohesion, so are the cells of the body of civilization, society, held together by a centripetal energy, adhesion, a more flexible law than the law of cohesion. And, just as a cell of the human body, failing to receive constantly an adequate supply of the proper food, failing to receive the constant renewing of its cells by the bath of life- sustaining food, diluted in the bloodstream, dies and weakens that portion of the human body; so with the cells of civilization, society, when they fail to get their required bath of life. sustaining blood, bearing in its liquid form food for the cells.

Some two hundred and fifty years ago Pope said: "Money is the lifeblood of Civilization," while Locke, even earlier, said, "If exportation will not balance importation, away must go your silver again, whether monied or not monied." In those two concise, congent statements, we find the complete purpose and danger of money.

Just as the bloodstream of the human body must perform two definite labours, if the body is to remain normal and healthy; so must the bloodstream of civilization. First. The bloodstream must carry the proper food in the proper amount to every cell of the body; and, Second. The bloodstream must carry away worn out and/or unneeded particles of food and of the body.

To carry this simile further: while money is the lifeblood of civilization, the banking system is the arteries and veins of the body of civilization through which this lifeblood flows. The two functions of banking — the keeping of the people's money on deposit together with the cashing and clearing of their cheques, and the lending of money, fit nicely into the figure of speech. The Treasury of the United States (ought to be), under the Constitution of the United States, is the heart of the blood system" while the banks are main arteries, and veins, and the depositing of money in the banks and the chequeing it out, is the network of capillaries breaking down the bloodstream and taking food to every particle of the body. This the banks fail to do consistently. Money lending is an aid to the process of growth, which adds new tissues to the body by swelling the bloodstream.

In other words, every human being in a social state has direct contact with the bloodstream, money, the use of it, that he may clothe, feed, shelter and entertain himself; and, conversely, as often as he has an excess of any human necessity or luxury, he must dispose of it and should receive for it money that he may keep his money stream normal and healthy; that he may spend money for what he has not. He must receive money for his excess, and the ideal condition obtains when he receives for his excess goods the exact amount required to buy the goods he lacks.

If he receives more than he spends, he shunts from the bloodstream that much which, if continued, will pile up ganglions of dead capital; and, just as with the human body, tumours, often cancerous, will form and interfere with the normal functioning of the entire body of civilization. Or, if he spends more money than he receives, soon the bloodstream will fail to carry to him, or another human being, maybe many, that food which their bodies must have if they remain normal and healthy. Just as tumours on the human body result finally in death to the entire body, unless expert surgery is employed; so does a tumour on the body of civilization tend to produce the death of civilization, unless expert surgery is employed in its removal.

If one segment of civilization, say a nation, sends out more money for goods than it takes in for goods sent out, it must ultimately find its bloodstream dried up, resulting in the death of that segment. And should it receive more money than it sends out, then tumours will form, and only expert surgery will prevent death.

In other words an excess of money is just as certain death to a normal and healthy human being, or to a segment of civilization, and many of its cells, as is a lack of it. Then our problem is to ascertain how we may keep the bloodstream of civilization filled with the proper amount of lifeblood: the needed portion for the cells' food supplied the outworn and unneeded particles removed: one building up, the other removing the debris.

That problem, can and must be solved. It can and will be solved by making proper adjustments in our modern money system. In these pages we shall undertake to indicate that solution.

For 168 years banks have been using two very unlike dollars: the earned dollar, and the phoney dollar.

The earned dollar was silver and gold coins. The miner laboured long and hard to mine and separate the gold and silver from the dross. He took it to the Government. The Government minted the gold into coins, and returned them to the miner at no cost to the miner — the "free coinage" practice. The Government could well afford to do that, because it provided the Government with metals which were in common use as money and they, in this act, obeyed the demand of the

Constitution that the "Congress ... shall coin money, and regulate the value thereof." They fixed the value of the coin at approximately the market value of the metal.

Gold and silver coins were *Earned Dollars*.

But finding the quantity of them too small, the Government, at the behest of bankers, began the practice of printing gold and silver certificates. This was not a thing of value, not a product of labour in the truest sense of the word, but a phoney "gold" and "silver" dollar added by the Government to swell the volume of money. It proved to be a wise thing to do under existing conditions; and since it was done by the Government for the people it was an act of the people, and immediately on the certificates being paid out to customers of the banks, and paid for products of labour, they became earned dollars. But when private banks, then National Banks, then Reserve Banks began to flood the country with private I.O.U.s, the earned dollar dropped into a very minor role in the money markets of the world. The earned dollar was just used for pocket and cash register change.

Had the government retained control of money and credit, and issued all paper money, and added all deposit credits on the books of the banks, limiting bankers — money lenders to the lending of the actual deposit credits they had in their own banks, together with such deposit credits as customers of the banks might have subrogated to them (as time deposits) no harm would have been done; but when the Reserve Act made corporation stock basis of bank reserves, which in turn became the source of bank credit, which was loaned to customers and thereby transformed into deposits, transferable by cheque with which customers of banks made over 90 percent of their monetary payments, the phoney dollar, the unearned dollar practically crowded the earned dollar out of the picture, and bankers were given the power of life and death over every person in the United States, by extending or withholding credit.

Producers of the material things people want and buy, together with those who serve others for hire, came up with their earned dollar, which amounted to a few billions, while the bankers shoved into the volume of money trillions of phoney dollars, which have competed with the earned dollar in the markets of the world. It reduced the earned dollar's buying power almost to nothing, and left the producer forced to continually fight for more pay that he might meet the high prices the phoney dollar has forced the sellers to demand.

Many definitions of money have been used, but the most accurate definition is "a medium of exchange."

In its true sense money is anything the seller will receive from the buyer in payment for his goods and/or services. It is always a promise to pay. In fact, money is a note the seller holds against the buyer.

But, before you may dignify a buyer's promise to pay as money, the promise must have the endorsement of the Government, that the seller may have the Government's guarantee that the promise to pay will be paid in full, and received by any seller. Therefore, the credit of the Nation must be pledged behind every dollar that the people may use and be assured that the money will be acceptable to all sellers.

Originally, our government minted gold and silver coin, products of labour, which had an intrinsic value, that is, a market value approximately equivalent to the stamped value of the coin. So the "guarantee" of the government was not imprinted on the coin, because the holder of the coin knew that the coin itself was worth the dollar; and that all sellers would receive it in payment for goods without question.

But as buying and selling increased, and the difficulty in keeping (from robbers) the gold and/or silver, and the transporting of it from buyer to seller became more and more difficult and hazardous, and even the quantity of it became inadequate, the Government began to engrave paper to be used in addition to coin.

This paper money, at the beginning, was gold Certificates, bearing the usual clause: "This certifies that there is on deposit in the Treasury of the United States of America Ten Dollars in gold payable to the bearer on demand." With the additional clause: "This certificate is legal tender for all debts, both public and private."

These statements were necessary because the odour of "continental currency" hung in the mental atmosphere so thickly that the people would not trust even the more stable Government of the United States.

Congressman John Sherman of Ohio chairman of the Banking Committee, on the passage of the National Bank Note Act, wrote the agents of the Rothschilds in New York:

"The Congress has passed your proposed Act, and it will become popular, and the people will accept it readily because it will look so much like Treasury Certificates. Very few citizens will understand the National Bank Notes Act, but those who do will be under such necessity of enjoying the banks' favours that they will say nothing about it, and the masses will bear the burden never knowing what it is all about."

That assertion is as true today as in the 70s when John Sherman wrote the letter.

But following the panics of 1873, 1893, and 1907, when banks failed and depositors lost billions of "money" deposits, a committee was appointed, at the behest of the bankers, to make a study of banking and money. When this committee made its report to Congress, the bankers introduced the Infamous Federal Reserve Act, which became a law with only six Congressmen and Senators voting against it; the others voted yes, and many of the leaders had been royally entertained at "Hobcaw", the 17,000 acre "Shangrila", owned by Bernard Baruch, a Doctor's son who went from rags to riches via the New York Stock Exchange.

The producers and servers laboured long hours' for their dollars. The bankers with the flick of a pen could create billions while the producers were earning hundreds.

Dollars are like spuds, the more you have of them, the less they will sell for; so every time banks add phoney money to the stream, it cheapens every earned dollar and unearned dollar, too. The only solution is for Congress to obey the Constitution, and take over the creation of money, deposit credits, which are transferable by cheque from buyer to seller; then keep the people's deposit accounts, cash and clear their cheques.

And keep this in mind, the $1,250 billion bank credits created in the issuing and selling $250 billion U.S. Bonds during World War II, was just as good money as the time deposits on the books, of the banks, and that sum, plus the $250 billion in bonds, gives a total of $1 trillion $500 billion dollars. All was a gift from the people of the United States of America; and as an added punishment for dumbness, we are having to pay $10 billion a year in interest.

I have said that the Federal Reserve Banking System has given us the most fluid money in the world; and that the commercial banks render the people of the United States a very great service:

(a)   in creating money (bank deposits);
(b)   in keeping the depositors' accounts;
(c)   in cashing and clearing their cheques; and

I have also said that all that they do is unconstitutional. It's their abuse which must we must stop.

To explain how they render those essential monetary services, would be easy, if you let me junk all the gobbledegook bankers use in running their business, and the page after page of "rules" they literally "have" Congress, pass as laws; and that is exactly what I shall do and have done.

In Chapter II, I have quoted from the Board of Governors of the Federal Reserve System's booklet, first printed in 1939, "THE FEDERAL RESERVE SYSTEM — Its Purposes and Functions," excerpts which succinctly tell the "how" the system functions ... I omit the purposes (almost) because they say nowhere and at no time the "real" purpose of banking. They always say: "Just trying to give the country a sounder money." And always repeating *"To control credit."*

I want you to read and re-read those lifted statements, given here with Chapter II, page 18, and try to see if you can get a clear picture of banking. It is pretty good, because those statements were made under the direction of the Reserve Board headed by Mariner S. Eccles, inoculated with the Dr. Roosevelt serum.

It was the first official serum administered to public officials which made them prone to put human rights above property rights; and these enlightening quotations should be memorized by you that you may understand what I shall say, and why.

There are two parties deeply involved in money: the buyer and the seller; there are two parties mixed up in the creation and control of money: the Government and Private Banking Corporations. There must always remain the buyer and seller, for money is an invention made by them, not as a measure of value but as an aid in the exchange of goods and services. The interests of buyer and seller are always antagonistic so the Government should act as umpire and call the plays.

There must not continue the co-partnership in creating and controlling money: the Government and banks. One must be eliminated, and the Constitution definitely eliminates the private banking corporations; therefore there *must be* only the Government in control of the creation of money, and fixing its purchasing power.

The first Article of the Constitution, and the very first Section says:

"All legislative powers herein granted SHALL BE vested in a Congress of the United States ... " Sections 2, 3, 4, 5, 6 and 7 constitute the Congress, and the 8th Section enumerates SPECIFICALLY the powers of Congress; and the first power mentioned is "money" "lay and collect taxes," and the second, "borrow Money,"

and the 5th:

"To coin money, regulate the value thereof, and of foreign coin, and fix the standard of weights and measures."

Memorize that section; for it must ever be in your mind, as you study banking, money, your place in the system.

I shall prove to you that we must eliminate the banking corporations from the creation, circulation, and control of money; and confine them to "lending only the deposit credits" to their credit on the books of the United States Depositories in absolute control of the Treasury of the United States, with the hand of Congress guiding every step and act in the business of providing the Nation its money supply — even the lending of deposits.

The trouble with bank deposits is that they are created in too large volume by private corporations for the corporations' gain, and incidentally usable as a "medium of exchange."

We have had this sort of money since Andy let Nick taunt him into killing the Second Bank of the United States, first in small quantities, as Gold and Silver. Even at that late date coins were shuttling about in an effort to meet the fluid demands of money; while today personal cheques are used in over 90 percent of our monetary payments.

We might wink at the Congress's farming out the public credit to private banking corporations, and giving them absolute (almost) control of the creation of money and the control of its circulation, and credit, if they did not hog the wealth of the Nation "with phoney money." Under the Federal Reserve Act, bankers, private corporations formed strictly for private gain, use the credit of the United States (its vast natural and material resources, its vast industrial and commercial activities, its resourceful planning, its eager, know-how man power, its, most democratic government poorly umpiring) to the hurt of the masses, the toiling, labouring, planning workers. The banking practices, given unlimited powers over money under the Federal Reserve Act, empowers them to expand or contract the flow of money at will, on a moment's notice, which either gives us "good times," or puts us in the bread line.

How true Ex-Congressman Callaway's statement to me in 1933: "I voted against the Federal Reserve Act of 1913, because it gives the bankers the power of life or death over every man, woman and child in the Nation."

The mechanics of money are so simple, when shorn of all the lengthy "red tape" bankers use to obscure money! The best money the world has discovered, as I have and shall often repeat, is "deposit credits, transferable by cheque, wherewith people make the bulk of their monetary payments." The Federal Reserve Act, which has just this year been "revised and amended," extending the red-tape obscurations, covering 252 pages, makes the creation of money a most mysterious thing.

Here are the essentials in that *best* money, which I shall reveal to you:

(1) A United States Depository in every community in the Nation,

(2) a set of books carrying the deposit credits of every person, firm or corporation served by that community's Depository,

(3) a staff of clerks and bookkeepers to administer the duties of the Depository,

(4) the Treasury of the United States as directing head, and

(5) the Congress of the United States. The course of cheques would be as follows, eliminating all clearing houses: John Doe in Austin would write a cheque to Joe Doak in any other community in the United States, in payment of a purchase Doe made from Doak. Doak would deposit it in his (local) depository; the depository would credit Doak's deposit account the face of the cheque, dollar for dollar, and mail the cheque to Doe's Depository in Austin, and Doe's Depository would debit Doe's account face of the cheque, dollar for dollar.

That would be the whole of the mechanics of that soundest and most fluid money the world has ever seen, if the Congressmen would quit perjuring themselves by taking an oath to support and uphold the Constitution, then turning around and violating that Constitution either witlessly or ignorantly.

The source of all deposit credits to the credit of the Government and the people, of course, will be Congress And the only way new deposit credits may get on these books will be by an order of Congress, and the new deposits will be written in the Depository's account by the Treasurer. Money's coming in from foreign countries, of course, will have to be handled by a special department of the Treasury, under rules laid down by Congress, that no additional deposit credits from any source other than from and through Congress, may enter the Nation's money stream.

There will be little bookkeeping required of the Depository's staff, other than crediting deposits to the depositor's account who hands, them cash or a cheque, or debiting another depositor's, account when a cheque he drew is presented to his depository. Of course they will keep an adequate supply of "United States tokens," money, on hand to cash cheques when presented and this will really be "cashing cheques," the transforming of deposits into currency. At the end of each day, each depository will send to the Treasury in Washington, a report of cheques cashed, deposits credited to customers, and deposits charged to depositors' accounts; and these reports will be quickly tabulated, and the Treasury will know how much money has been chequed out (or received by each and all Depositories in the Nation) , and where the deposits are, Depository to Depository, and ,the grand total of these each day must be the same as the grand total of the day before; for under the Treasury control and administration of the Depositories it is important that, no deposits can appear or disappear, without the fact being conveyed to the Treasury, then to Congress.

One of the major objectives of the Congress will be to keep the supply of money constant from day to day. The constant volume of deposits transferable by cheque, will maintain a constant value of the dollar; for dollars are like spuds, the more you have of them (the nation as a whole) the less the dollar will buy; and the only value you can give a dollar, is its purchasing power.

The Gold dollar coin never did that; nor any other fiat dollar. Only volume controls.

That is exactly why the wise men who wrote the Constitution of the United States couched in the same "power" both the coining of money, and the fixing of the standard of weights and measures.

To tell me that a gold dollar has so many grains of gold is of no interest to me, because I do not intend to use the metal. My only purpose would be to use it to buy a commodity, say coffee.

The bankers still say that the standard value of our dollar is gold; yet in 1943, before World War II dragged us in, you could buy four pounds of coffee for $1.08; now one pound of coffee will cost you $1.09; so in '43 the gold dollar was worth four times what it is today, in the coffee market of the world. How absurd. And Uncle Sam is still paying $35 an ounce for gold.

The defenders of "creditalism" say that coffee costs more to deliver it to the customer ... always, they say, "because wages went up — the damned union!"

And the Union replies that we had to have more because what we bought cost more ... on ad infinitum ... to nausea.

When Congress controls volume of dollars, if a dollar would buy a bushel of wheat today, a dollar would buy a bushel of wheat August 19, 1997; for the relationship and the relative values of the deposit dollar and the commodity for sale, would not change. So in the end the value of the dollar would be fixed in terms of corn, wheat, spuds, tuna fish, or what have you; and when once fixed, it could not fluctuate; for if it did, then my dollar which could not fluctuate in volume and therefore purchasing power, would not buy my necessities.

The high priest of fluctuating values, Bernard Baruch, and the patron god of the Federal Reserve System, which pours new deposit money into the deposit reservoirs in a constant flood; and has been doing it in ever increasing flood volume since their complete bust in 1933, and their reshoring the dykes with legislation in 1934, says now, in today's *Saturday Evening Post*:

"... my experience as chairman of the War Industries Board in World War One taught (me) that if 'inflation were to be prevented in a second war, a ceiling has to be imposed on all prices, wages, rents and profits at the very start of the emergency. (But every day is an emergency.) But when World War II started, both President Franklin Roosevelt and Congress decided to 'wait and see.' The necessary over-all ceilings were not imposed for two years and then only after the inflationary race was on. The same process of wait and see was repeated in the Korean War." If price ceilings in war times, why not in peace times?

Barney had his mind on what his dollar would not buy, and wanted to lay the whole blame on the price the seller charged. He wanted to continue his stream of new dollars, and then have the Congress and President compel people to take his cheap dollar at the old (in the 30's price level) dollar's buying power.

CHAPTER VII

SIMPLIFIED MECHANICS OF RESERVE BANKING

I have quoted many men — giving their opinions and observations about banking, money. I have printed excerpts from the book issued by the 1939 Board of Governors of the Federal Reserve System — *The Federal Reserve System — Its Purposes and Functions.* I have given many details of the functions of the Federal Reserve System. I have said little about the purposes of the Reserve System, for there is little to say, and that is that The Federal Reserve System was created by an act of Congress, at the behest of bankers, for the purpose of giving bankers absolute control of this country, and of giving them title to the wealth of the Nation. (But that, of course, is not mentioned in The Reserve Act.)

A bank is a private corporation incorporated for the purpose of making money. It has no humanitarian purpose to serve. It holds no interest in the general welfare of the country, other than the farmer has in his mules. It looks upon persons as cogs in a giant industrial wheel, whose every turn must make them richer and richer. It is a person in the sense that the Supreme Court of the United States declared a corporation a "person." It is nerveless, conscious-less, unmerciful, domineering, wholly destructive, and as dishonest and ruthless as any pirate that ever sailed the seven seas.

I have not undertaken to delineate its mechanics beyond its creation and control of money and credit.

While its activities in every phase of our monetary life affect the lives of all of us, we have in mind only the mechanics which create our money, control our money and our credit. In brief, I am interested only in returning, the creation of money, and the regulating the value thereof, to the hands of Congress.

Let me enumerate the steps taken in the Reserve Banks in the creation of credit, the transmuting the credit into bank deposits, and the cashing and clearing of cheques drawn against these bank deposits.

First, The Reserve authorities create bank reserves.

Second, Reserve Bank credits are convertible into commercial bank credit.

Third, Commercial bank credit is convertible into bank deposits to the credit of borrowers from the banks, or sellers who sell to the banks investment obligations.

Those are the three steps in the creation of "bank deposits transferable by cheque wherewith business men and other persons make the bulk of their monetary payments.".

On page 55, Federal Reserve System booklet, we find:

"Loans and purchases of securities by the Federal Reserve authorities are one of the important sources of member bank reserves."

These securities may be U.S. Bonds, corporation stock, notes, mortgages, debentures, any investment obligation. When the Reserve authorities buy corporation stock, they give a cheque against no funds in payment for the stock, and the corporation deposits this cheque with its home bank. This creates bank deposits; then when the cheque reaches the bank's Reserve Bank, the Reserve Bank gives the member bank credit in its reserve fund the face of the cheque, dollar for dollar. One cheque created two funds: bank deposits, and bank credit.

In depositing the Reserve authorities' cheque in a member bank it reversed the order of creation of credits. First the cheque created bank deposits; then it created an equal amount of bank reserves; then the next step is with the commercial member bank — it multiplies its reserves by 5. It makes loans, or buys investment obligations, giving the borrowers and the sellers deposit credits on their books, new bank deposits.

And that's the whole picture. Of course there are many different purchases the Reserve authorities may make, but it matters not what they may buy, when they give the seller a cheque, when it is deposited, it creates both new bank deposits and new bank reserves. And this is true: every time a Government cheque is deposited, it creates bank deposits; but only when the cheque is given by the government against new deposit credits it got on the books of the Reserve Banks when selling anew issue of bonds, does the cheque create new deposit credits.

Cheques given by the Government against revenue funds which come in from the taxpayers merely restore to the people the bank deposits transferred from the taxpayers' account to the Government's deposit account in taxes.

Let's take a typical case and trace the steps: The Reserve authorities buy in the open market $10 million corporation stock. That is step one. The corporation deposits the cheque in its home bank and this creates $10 million bank deposits. This is step two. The member bank sends the Reserve cheque to its Reserve Bank, and the Reserve Bank credits the member bank's reserve account $10 million. Then a fourth step is taken. The $10 million reserve credit to the account of the member bank which the member bank multiplies by five, giving it a $50 million bank credit, and on lending this it is converted into $50 million bank deposits. Added to the corporation's deposits of $10 million, gives us $60 million new bank deposits.

Probably the corporation made no improvement in machinery or plant, but spent the money in riotous living. It became, however, a liability against the future production of the plant, for the U.S. Supreme Court has held that a corporation is entitled to six percent return on its investment. The corporation was $10 million richer, for the stock was put on the stock exchange, and became the property of stockholders, who may never receive a dividend, and finally the stock may become worthless because the corporation fails in business. But in such cases the stockholder has no recourse. He must write off his stock as loss. But if it succeeds, the consumers of the corporation's goods must pay an additional amount of $600,000, as dividends on this $10,000,000 new corporation stock. And when the bank collects the $50 million it loaned against the $10 million bank reserves, it will be $60 million richer in bank deposits.

Every time the United States sells a new issue of bonds, the same mechanics result in the same creative processes.

For example, when Congress voted $250 billion to pay costs of World War II, just as any other borrower would do the Secretary of the Treasury laid the bonds, which are government notes, on the Reserve Bank's desk. The Reserve Bank gave the Government a $250 billion deposit credit. (Of course the whole set of bonds were not sold at one time, but when all were sold to the Reserve Banks, the final deposit credits were $250 billions.)

When the Government chequed the $250 billion out to pay for goods and services, the government cheques were deposited in commercial banks, and the total cheques created $250 billion new deposit credits in commercial banks. When 'the cheques reached the several banks: Reserve Banks, the member banks sending the Government cheques for clearing, got $250 billion new reserves to the credit of their reserve accounts.

These funds on the books of the Reserve Banks to the credit of member banks are "reserve funds," but when thought of on the books of the member banks, they are "member bank credits," which member banks can use in making loans or in buying investment obligations. Usually all banks may lend an average of five times their reserve funds; however, the Reserve authorities may change the percentages at any time.

Remember that the buying of the $250 billion U.S., Bonds created ultimately $1 trillion — $250 billion bank credits. Suppose the member banks should make loans and buy investment obligations (and maybe they have done so) equal to the entire amount of their bank credits, then they would create $1 trillion, $250 billion new bank deposits ($1,250,000,000,000). That sum is many times more than the physical value of all the property, real estate, and goods, and manpower, too in the Nation. So in financing the Second World War, bankers with a flick of the pen, created enough bank deposits, to buy the whole United States many times.

Let's see what the issuing of $250 billion in U.S. Bonds did for our money supply:

> U.S. Bonds, which will draw interest from here on out. $250 billion
> Reserve Bank Deposits to the credit of The United States. $250 billion
> Reserve Bank reserves to the credit of the member banks. $250 billion
> Member Bank Credit, which they may use to buy investment obligations or make loans $1,250 billion
> Member Bank Deposits to the credit of their depositors subject to cheque. $1,250 billion
> Investment obligations owned by the member banks. $1,250 billion
> An Infamous Total. $3,000 billion

In all of my tables, I have sought an idea and the figures are only approximately true... Our National debt today is approximately $276 billion, and the Congress is raising the debt limit to $280 billion, in anticipation of nuclear wars.

Of course, Reserve Bank reserves and member bank credits are not actual money, transferable by cheque. They are fictitous "funds" bankers keep on their books, as basis of loans, but funds which they use to buy investment obligations. So they are "cash" to banks. And these fictitious funds cost the bankers nothing, except the trouble of keeping the people's deposits, cashing and clearing their cheques ... the cash cost them nothing, and the clearing of the cheques, is just a bookkeeping routine, performed by underpaid men and women.

Let's look at that again. The Reserve authorities did not use cash, anyone's deposits, to pay Uncle Sam for these bonds. The Washington Reserve Bank wrote on its deposit books deposit credits to the Government, $250 billion; the Government wrote a total of $250 billion in cheques to those who worked for the Government, or sold it goods — this transferred the $250 billion to the people; the banks where these cheques were deposited (or cashed) sent the cheques to each bank's Reserve Bank, and the Reserve Bank gave the bank credit in its Reserve Fund for the cheques, all totalling $250 billion; the member banks had their reserves increased that amount, so that increased their bank funds (credits) to $1,250 billion.

When the $1,250 billion has been loaned, as it could be and may have been - there is no way of MY finding out; and Congress seems not to be interested - there will appear in the vaults of the banks $1,250 billion in notes, mortgages, vendors lien notes, corporation stock and other investment obligations. The depositors are using (if they could) the deposits they got for their notes or investment obligations.

So we find that there are $250 billion U.S. Bonds which are actual money; $250 billion Bank Deposits which were given the Government for the Bonds; and the $1,250 billion deposits to the credit of the people who borrowed or sold to the banks investment obligations. These three moneys, totalling $1,750 billion remain in active (or nascent) state. As often as the bankers re- sell an investment obligation, they transfer to their books a portion of those $1,250 billion bank deposits, and when all notes are paid or all investment obligations are sold, the banks then will have the entire $1,250 billion new bank deposits on their side of the ledger. And they have the bonds — Total $1,500 million!

It is an endless chain, forged with three links, endlessly repeated: (1) create bank reserves; (2) lend Bank credit; (3) which creates bank deposits. The forging of these three colourful links go on every banking hour, year in and year out, as the chain about our necks grows longer and longer, ever recoiling around our necks; until now economic death is written on every slave's face.

All these steps are just the hocus pocus of the sleight of hand artist, who must move the shell from hand to hand so quickly that the eye cannot follow the movements, and at once the victim becomes confused and actually must "guess" under which shell is the quarter.

Bankers will not say that deposits cancel out; they will only say, if they say anything, that these deposits "tend to cancel out."

Too at any time the bank may buy investment obligations, and perhaps pay for them by chequeing against the bank's undivided profits but banks have forgotten how to pay cash or their own deposits for investment obligations. They always pay for them by giving the seller deposit credits to his account; which increases the total deposits of the bank.

Bank deposits have accumulated in such vast sums to the credit of the bankers, that they have entered the "loansharks' field." In every town and city many "finance companies" have opened offices, and are lending money supplied to them by the banks who own them. They are using the same methods the parent loansharks have always used.

During the last few years lending offices, finance companies, have opened throughout the Nation, many in every town. These are departments of banks, through which bankers are now siphoning their actual deposits" not new deposits" into the people's pockets. The banks in this fashion have entered the loanshark field, and are practicing the same sort of robbery that the hole-in-the-wall loansharks have been practicing only these new finance agencies use dignified terms to cover their usurious practices, never the obnoxious term "interest."

Cost of investigating the borrowers' responsibilities, expense of making small loans, on and on; and interest is not mentioned. They don't have the borrower sign a note any more, they present him a "loan agreement" which the borrower signs, with the unctuous statement, "here is your cheque, we will complete filling in the agreement (the terms of which have not been discussed), and mail them to you in a few days."

When the nineteen men who met in New York City to ponder our money supply back in the early fifties, the problem they pondered was, a double header: (a) What are we going to do with the hundreds of billions of deposit dollars we have piled up since World War II? (b) Must we stop the pumps and begin to siphon this excess money off.

So they ordered the interest rate increased and informed their customers that "The Government will not let us make that sort of loan." They always say the "Government won't let us do that." When as a matter of fact, they tell the Government what it can do and never bother about what the Government may think about what they do.

These 19 men had put on the squeeze, and today the little fellow can't get money at the banks' main loan desk; he has to go to another building and get a loan from an agency of the bank, and pay 50 percent of the total loan as "carrying charges."

Ask a bank if it is behind or owns that lending agency, and he will blandly say, "Why, of course not we are in the money lending business ourselves."

But back to the results of the chain of actions and reactions the issuing of $250 billion U.S. Bonds had on the volume of money following World War II. We will suppose the volume of bank deposits (time and demand deposits) at the beginning of the war was $33,360,000,000. By 1947 these deposits had increased to $108,500,000,000, or over 300 percent. That represents only time and demand deposits to the accounts of customers of banks.

Lending has been wild since 1947, as the Korean War shot new blood into the industrial and economic arteries, and a building boom and industrial expansion that has astounded the world has been financed by additions to the bank deposits; and no one knows the total added.

Each Bond they sold transferred deposits from the customers' deposit accounts to the bankers'; and the bankers could then spend these deposits, after declaring dividends, and buy anything they wanted. It was another "trick" of the bankers. For profit.

Let me prove that by citing two instances: An oil friend (millionaire many times) said to me (this was in December, 1943):

"I was in my banker's office (the First National Bank of Dallas) talking to the president of the bank. I remarked, 'Well, I guess I must be patriotic, and buy some bonds.'"

The president of this *great* bank said, "If you have cash and want to invest it, buy first mortgage notes, land or other good investment obligations. Don't buy bonds. The Government has all the money it needs, and can get more if it needs it. However, if you want your neighbours to think that you have done your bit, buy bonds in $100,000 or $200,000 blocks, give us your note for that amount; we will attach your (?) bonds to the note for security, clip the coupons for our interest; and in a few weeks we will mark your note paid, and return it to you."

Well, we little fellows are quick (sometimes) to catch on. I knew that the banks were selling their own U.S. Bonds, but I didn't know you could buy them without chequeing against your existing deposits. Of course, the banks don't divulge those facts to little fellows.

So a few days before the bond sale, I said to the cashier of the local bank, "Bob I want to have it announced that the 'Baird Star' has bought a $1,000 bond." Bob replied, "Well, go ahead and buy it; you have ample cash to pay for it."

"But," I replied, "I need that cash to operate my paper. This is what I want you to do: let me sign a $1,000 note; you attach the bond to the note as your security; keep the note as long as you want to; clip the coupons for your interest, and when you want to mark my note paid, keep the bond as payment; and send me the note."

With surprise in his eyes, he looked at me a moment and said, "Maybe I could not do that as a banker!" And I replied, "Do you want me to explain to you why and how you can?" Searching my face for a moment, he picked up a blank promissory note, filled it in for

$1,000, and I signed it. He kept the note, and handed me a deposit slip. I walked to the teller's window, and wrote a cheque against that deposit slip in favour of the bank and handed it to the teller in payment for the bond.

I never saw the bond. I was announced at the bond sale as the purchaser of a $1,000 bond. In a few days I got the note marked paid.

When my note returned to me, I had lost nothing nor gained anything. But the banker owned the bond to begin with he had paid for it by having the Reserve Banks, who first bought the bonds from the Government by giving the Government deposit credits on their books, charge the cost of the bond against the bank's reserve, and this reserve account had cost the Baird bank nothing. Now he owned the $1,000 deposit credits which he and I created in the act of my borrowing and his making the loan; and the bank, after declaring a dividend could allocate that $1,000 to the several stockholders, and the $1,000 went back into demand deposits, to buy anything the stockholders might want.

Now let's analyse that incident: When I signed the note, and was handed a deposit slip, the act of creating a new $1,000 bank deposit was completed. That night, when the banker posted his books, they showed that his bank had $1,000 more deposits. When I handed the banker the note, and he attached the bond, the bank was richer by $1,000. My note created the $1,000 in new deposit credits, and when I chequed these deposits over to the bank, then the bank had the bond, my note, and the $1,000 deposits. All done in 20 minutes.

So, on and on, they sell bonds, and get existing deposit credits; and buy the bonds back, getting them simply by adding new deposits to the sellers' account. When a bank buys a U.S. Bond, it is buying an investment obligation; therefore it pays for it with new deposits, and the "aggregate bank deposits are increased." When it buys your note, a mortgage, a U.S. Bond, corporation stock, any form of investment obligation it pays for all and each of them by giving the seller new deposits.

In summation the whole story boils down to this: Bankers buy your note and other investment obligations, and pay for them by giving you new deposits on their books. When you buy your note back, pay the note off, you cheque over to the banker your deposits, and he credits them to' the bank's account. That is the whole sum and substance of lending money, and buying investment obligations. The bankers use a lot of gobbledegook explaining what they do and then turn to the Congress of the United States to have it write a set of rules as a cover up... the last one written and passed this year, covers 250 pages. But shorn of all of the camouflage, the rules of banking are: Buy notes and other investment obligations, and pay with new deposits; sell notes and other investment obligations, and take deposit credits for them. Pay nothing for what they get; get cash for what they sell.

Of course, readers, I know that as you read you are saying, "But that can't be true; bankers couldn't make money that fast; and of course I have cash on deposit;

why if the banker got the depositors' deposits every time they hand cash out to customers, and then created new deposits every time the depositors hand cash back to them — why in a few days these banks would be bursting with their own money — nope, it's my cash and the banker just hands it out to me free, and takes it back to keep it safe for me."

And some of you are going to persist in believing all the lies and clichés bankers have fed you on, and refusing to believe what anyone else says about banking.

The facts of their multiplying, creating money out of thin air remains, whether you admit it or not.

If all monetary values-bank deposits, time and demand, and bank surpluses, deposits, those shown in bank statements, and those not shown, were in $1.00 bills, the banks' vaults and whole buildings would be bursting with them; but you must understand that these monetary values are just figures on the books of banks, dormant and unseen, until you write a cheque and give it to a seller for his goods and/or services. It takes a very few seconds to write $1,000,000,000, or even $1,000,000,000,000 on a page of the bank ledger; and one page would hold many entries; so one sheet of paper can evidence billions of monetary values to the credit of many persons.

Congress, by laws they passed, assigned to the banks the credit of the Nation, gratis; then it empowered the Reserve authorities to write a cheque against no funds, and buy investment obligations, which gave the banks both title to the investment obligations, and reserve funds. At every step the banks "created" the funds they used; and the member banks came into possession of the reserve funds created by the Reserve authorities without ever knowing where the reserve funds came from, simply through the act of accepting cheques drawn against Reserve Bank deposits, for deposit in their banks. The reserve funds not only did not cost the member banks one thin dime, they did not promise the depositors of these cheques which increased their share of the reserve funds to their credit on the books of the Reserve but two things: (a) to cash their cheques, (b) to clear their cheques. At no time did they have to pay for the cash they got or the reserves they enjoyed: just promised to do simple bookkeeping for their customers — to keep their monetary accounts.

Free Reserve credits; free member bank reserve funds; free member bank credit; and they sold these free bank credits to customers and got investment obligations in exchange, and when these investment obligations were paid off, or re-sold, they got bank deposits to their credit. "Unsound," you say. "Impossible," you shout. "The Government would not tolerate that," you reason.

Well, gentle readers, *your* government does. Your Congressmen, by perjuring themselves, in violation of the oaths of office they took, which were "to support, uphold, and defend the Constitution of the United States," passed banking laws written by bankers, culminating in the just passed "S.1451," an act to amend and revise the statutes governing financial institutions and credit.

That Act consolidates all banking laws passed by Congress through the years, deleting some, adding much. It covers 252 pages, and uses 100,000 words. It puts forth as much effort to obscure and confuse its meaning, as it does to state the "purposes and functions" of banking. But it does do some terrible things. (a) It surrenders to private banking corporation the nation's credit; (b) it, therefore, compels the Government to pay the bankers interest to use its own (originally) credit-it thereby makes the banking corporation the master of the Government, of the nation; (c) it provides that bankers need have no funds (cash or property) to lend, or to use in buying investment obligations; (d) it provides that customers' deposits shall govern the extent of their loans, but serve no part in making loans; (e) it sets up a chain-reaction of bank financing which gives them *Free, Reserve Bank* credit, member bank reserves (on the books of the Reserve Banks), member bank credits, which they lend to customers, or use in buying investment obligations.

The Act, S.1451, completes the rape of the nation, and completes the surrender of the entire Nation its wealth, its industries, its man power, its destiny - to bloodless, soulless, conscienceless, corrupt, thieving persons — corporations, incorporated for gain, gain only. Remember that Sir Josiah Stamp, in the 20's, then the President of the World's most powerful bank, the Bank of England, and the second richest man in the British empire said:

"Banking was conceived in iniquity, and born in sin... The bankers own the earth. Take it away from them, but leave them the power to create money and control credit, and with a flick of the pen they will create enough money to buy it back again. Take this power away from them, and all great fortunes like mine would disappear. They ought to disappear. This would give us a better and a happier world to live in. BUT, if you want to continue the slaves of bankers, and pay the cost of your own slavery, then let them continue to create money and control credit... However, so long as governments will legalize such things, a man is foolish not to be a banker."

Financial Institutions Act Of 1957
A Legal Monstrosity — S.1451 — An Act
To amend and revise the statutes governing financial institutions and credit

Page 29. Article 34, (6) (A) (The total obligations to any national banking association of any person, co-partnership, association, or corporation shall at no time exceed 10 percentum of the amount of the capital stock of such association actually paid in and unimpaired and 10 percentum of unimpaired surplus fund ... Such limitation of 10 percentum shall be subject to the following exceptions:)

"(6) (A) Obligations of any person, co-partnership, association or corporation, in the form of notes or drafts secured by shipping documents, warehouse receipts, or other such documents transferring or securing title covering readily marketable non-perishable staples when such property is fully covered by insurance, if it is customary to insure such staples, shall be subject under this section to a limitation of 15 percentum of such capital and surplus in addition to such 10 percentum of such capital and surplus when the market value of such staples securing such additional obligation is not at any time less than 115 percentum of the face amount of such obligation, and to an additional increase of limitation of five percentum of such capital and surplus in addition to such 25 percentum of such capital and surplus when the market value of such staples securing such additional obligations is not at any time less than 120 percentum of the face amount of such additional obligation, and to a further additional increase of limitation or five percentum of such capital and surplus in addition to such 30 percentum of such capital and surplus when the market value of such staples securing such additional obligation is not at any time less than 125 percentum of the face amount of such additional obligation, and to a further additional increase of limitation of five percentum of such capital and surplus in addition to such 35 percentum of such capital and surplus when 'the market value of such staples securing such additional obligation is not at any time less than 130 percentum of the face amount of such additional obligation, and to a further additional increase of limitation of five percentum of such capital and surplus in addition to such 40 percentum of such capital and surplus when the market value of such staples securing such additional obligation is not at any time less than 135 percentum of the face amount such additional obligation, and to a further additional increase of limitation of five percentum of such capital and surplus in addition to such 45 percentum of such capital and surplus when the market value of such staples securing such additional obligation is not at any time less than 140 percentum of the face amount of such additional obligation, but this exception shall not apply to obligation of anyone person, co- partnership, association, or corporation arising from the same transaction and secured by the identical staples for more than ten months."

Gentle reader, I have quoted that 350-word paragraph (plus the parenthesized sentences preceding same as introductory to the paragraph) to indicate how industriously the bankers seek to camouflage and muddy their legal waters. They used 100,000 words in this latest act they compelled Congress to enact into law, and the President had no other course, for as they defied President Truman when he appealed to them to not let market price of U.S. Bonds drop below par, they could have visited reprisals upon the Government itself in such force that there was no other course for a supine Congress and a pliant President to do but pass the act and sign it.

Now let's see how few words the writers of the Constitution of the United States would have used:

"(6) (A) The obligation shall be subject under this section covering title to readily marketable non-perishable staples to a limitation of 10 percent if the market value of the staples is 100 percent of the obligation, 25% if 115%, 30% if 120%,35% if 125%, 40% if 130%, 45% if 135%, and 50% if 140% of the face amount of such additional obligation." That's just 59 words, which do the work of 350!

And as I have been writing those paragraphs, laboriously, because it is almost impossible to keep the mind on the word following the preceding one, there has been running through my deeper mind that statement of the old Roman Tacitus who said "When a nation is most corrupt, laws most multiply;" and today with our speedwriters, they run into 100,000 words!.

It is an axiom in equity and human understanding that any law that a common citizen, with a reasonable ability to read, cannot understand is a bad law. Suppose the Coach wrote a set of rules of the game not one of his players could understand, how could they get the commands?

CHAPTER VIII

THE HAND OF THE BANKER

TRACING A SORDID SCROLL

In 1942, a young father of 32, volunteered for naval duty in World War II, and served until V-J Day in 1945, serving the last 18 months of the War in the thick of Japan's, Kamikaze type of warfare, having his ship hit by a suicide plane, then watching the crew turn the hose on, washing the blood and bits of the Jap from the shattered deck. He rose from raw recruit to rank of Lieutenant Commander. He had spent the previous seven years in government service in Washington. He reached home in October 1945. He spent a few days in Marshall with his wife and daughter. He had no property, no established business, no credit, and little money. He did not want to go back to Washington, although he had been offered $6,000 a year job, if he would return. He had promised himself while hourly facing mutilation on the Pacific, that if he returned from this carnage, he would build the dream of his boyhood and youth, a print shop, patterned on the Roycrofters of East Aurora N.Y., and that he would build near the University of Texas. So he came to Austin to look the possibilities over.

In 1932, a man in his 40's who had made a start in the oil game in Ranger oil boom, went to East Texas field. He was worth about $100,000. He installed a small refinery. He was one of the lucky few. He survived the efforts of the major oil companies, aided and abetted by the Governor of Texas, the Texas Rangers, the Attorney General of Texas, the Comptroller of Texas, the Oil and Gas Commission of Texas, the city banks of Texas, the banks of Cleveland, San Francisco St. Louis, Chicago and New York, every little bribed constable of Texas, the National Guard (officered by employees of the majors) of Texas, District Courts of Texas, legions of smart lawyers in Texas, in Washington and in New York — to kill the small oil operators and small refineries in the oilfields of East Texas. Not because he was a good fighter, but because the major oil companies chose him, along with a few more small operators, to survive.

One afternoon, a Standard Oil Company official walked into this oil man's little office in an old cottage on his refinery grounds, and said: "We don't want to kill all the little refineries. The public would shout monopoly. So we must have a few to play against that cry. We have killed most of them but there are still too many. Why don't you buy one of them?"

This oil man asked, "What would I use for money?" "We'll honour your draft."

"Well, I have a $30,000 note due tomorrow at the First National Bank in Dallas. When you came in I was wondering where I would get enough money to pay it off."

The Standard official walked to the door, called to his Secretary who left the big polished Cadillac, and with a brief case under his arm, entered the little oil office. In fifteen minutes the small oil man had a $30,000 draft on

the Chase National Bank, New York. The little oil man
had arrived. He had been accepted by the majors. A few
weeks later an issue of his little company's stock
appeared on the New York Stock Market. Yep. It had
been bought in the "open market" by the Reserve
Authorities. The little oil man was entering the big oil
man's sphere. He walked into the First National Bank
of Dallas a little jauntier than he had with the $30,000,
and deposited to his account the million-dollar cheque
the Reserve authorities had given him. He returned to
his little office. He began to buy producing wells. He
began buying leases and drilling. His refinery grew. He
was growing BIGGER. Oil money poured in and he
began buying ranches and farms-safe investments,
14,000-acre ranch here, 500 acre farm there. The war
came. He said conscription is right. A man should be
compelled to fight for his country! His black gold
flowed *in bigger and ever BIGGER STREAMS, piling up
bigger and ever BIGGER profits.* He bought more and
more real estate. He felt grateful.

With millions of oil money coming in his desire for real
estate outran the stream of oil money. Real estate began
to double and double again in the sales price. Others
were making their thousands and millions. A feeling
that money was hot sent everybody scurrying about for
a "safe investment," and only real estate seemed safe.
He found banks would lend *big* money, in the hundreds
of thousands at two percent, on good revenue-bearing
property, on long-time note, secured only by deed of
trust on the property. He found he could buy interest in
a big hotel for

$650,000. The banker said, "OK." He filled in a note and a deed of trust, the millionaire signed them and handed them back to the banker, and the banker gave him a deposit slip for $650,000. He handed cheque to seller of hotel. No cash was touched. No existing deposits were touched. The banker and the borrower actually created $650,000. Only six figures were written on the bank's books. The banker handed a clerk a carbon deposit slip and he entered $650,000 to the credit of the oil man. The recipient of the cheque deposited it and a clerk credited his account $650,000 and in turn debited the oil man's account $650,000. *And the total bank deposits were increased* $650,000!

The veteran found he must build a cottage first. This rich oil man is his friend. He turned to him, and he readily endorsed the veteran's loan at the bank.

One had made millions out of the War, while the other came out of the War poorer, with three of the best years of his life lost. Both stood before a banker for a loan.

Both had rendered service to their nation in time of stress. One had been rewarded in many goods. The other had only an honourable discharge. So it seems that when weighed on even a banker's balances the beam would be perfectly horizontal, maybe tilted a little in recognition of the veteran's necessity as well as his active service in arms.

But a banker is a banker. He let the oil man who did not need a hotel have $650,000 at 2%, with many years to pay it back, if ever! He let the veteran have $3,000 at

6% to build a home, and $2,500 at 6% to buy an offset press, with the oil man's endorsement of the loan, yet the bankers demanded that the veteran pay in full in 18 months!

The Crimes the Loans Set Going

But that is not the end of the long criminal trail the banker opened up. Loans were not made with the bank's surplus, or undivided profits, or stock holders' funds. Nor was a single dollar of the depositors loaned. The $650,000 was actually *created* and added to the banker's total deposits, to go out and compete with every depositor's dollar, lowering every dollar's purchasing power. If there were $6,500,000 on deposit in the bank it reduces the purchasing power 10 percent. Dollars are like spuds: the more there are, the less they are worth. And all the 14,567 banks are making loans, so the ratio for the country as a whole is approximately the same.

But the trail of crime does not end there. The sellers of the hotel buy ranches, farms, other real estate. All know we have too much money, that it's getting cheaper every day. They're seeking safe investment. Land always offers the safest of all. Knowing the money is cheap. Knowing another 1929 to 1935 is certain, only the finale will be different. Probably multiplied billions of bank deposits, including theirs, will be wiped out. The farmer sells. Finds he can't buy as good farm for twice the price. He joins the houseless howling mobs in towns and cities, worrying as high prices eat away his life's savings.

But that's not the end of this cruel, selfish crime trail. Those hotel owners are not the sort who will till the soil, feed the stock. They remain in town, hire men (usually) to build good fences, padlock the gate and flee to the hills that their rotten hides may be cooled. While the poor man who would till the soil and slop the hogs can not buy the high-priced land, and ever hope to pay for it, and feed his family.

Cheap, inflated money robs farmers of their farms, the producers of their goods, the workers of their food and clothing, the aged of their pensions, crying babes of their bottle of milk.

But bankers, gamblers and dealers in the miseries of men, take the land, corner the products of labour, and weld about the ankles of the toiling sweating, producing masses, of even the babies shackles of bondage for another 100 years.

"The People Shall Rise up,"

Said Congressman Wright Patman, on December 1 , 1943, "One of these days the people of this country are going to rise up in their wrath and compel the change of such an idiotic system that compels our own people to pay tribute to a few who have nothing invested and run no risk, in order to conduct the affairs of our Government, and especially our national defence program. If some person attempts to show how the credit of the Nation is being farmed out *free* to "14,567" privately owned commercial banks he could be (is) quickly silenced by a whispering campaign that he is a monetary nut, a crackpot, or a greenbacker who wants to flood the country with printing-press money. Then a few references to continental currency, fiat money, and German inflation, and the opposition is dead."

The Dallas News and other corporation owned and controlled papers, journals and magazines were saying those very things about Patman, because he was fighting for non-interesting bearing War Bonds, and even the Chairman R.L. Doughton of the Ways and Means (meaning-ways and means to rob the people) Committee, objecting to Patman's saying:

"I'm opposed to the United States Government, which possesses the sovereign and exclusive authority to *create* and *control* money, paying private bankers for its own money. These private bankers do not lend their own money to the Government; they lend only the Government's money to the Government, and collect an interest charge on it annually."

If the Government were not paying any interest on this *money* the Government is borrowing, how would you get the banks to lend the money? They say, *"It is the money of our depositors,* we are responsible for it, and if we don't get anything for the use of it, we will not buy the bonds."

Doughton knew that he was: repeating an age-old lie bankers whine to every person to whom they don't want to lend money, and truly all such misinformed men should be kicked out of Congress.

At the same hearing Patman said:

"The total capital stock in the 14,567 commercial banks (national, state and private) amounts to only $3,500,000,000, and surplus and undivided profits to $5 billion more, and the total capital stock of 12 Reserve banks is only $150,000,000.

Said:

To fool the people, 'The right of selling bonds directly to the Reserve Banks by the Treasury is authorized by the Second War Act, enacted March 27, 1942, is limited to $5 billion. However, it does not prevent Reserve Banks buying $100,000,000,000 or $200,000,000,000 through the open Market Committee in N.Y.'"

And Patman should have added; it matters not to whom the Treasury of the United States turns over the Government bonds, they find their way to some bank, and when they do bankers CREATE NEW DEPOSITS TO PAY for them, which increases the Nation's aggregate deposits: so why quibble over which bank gets them first?

Patman continued:

"Why should we burden the people with a 300-billion dollar debt, when *we know* they will never be able to pay more than just the interest on it? That means a *perpetual debt* of $300 billion! That means that any inflation that we have in that $300 billion will remain indefinitely. Should you save the interest, $6 billion a year, the interest would pay the $300 billion off in only 50 years."

And he might have added: Inasmuch as the $300 billion was a direct gift from the Government to the banks, they should be willing to hold them for a 50 year instalment cash-payment settlement.

Patman continued:

"It was reported, January, 1943, that the 20 largest banks in the United States, twelve of them in New York City, held Government bonds at the end of 1942 to the amount of $16,407,197,000. The people will pay them between 300 and 400 million dollars interest a year. The National Government is sovereign because it has no government over it. It has the power to create its own credit upon which no interest should be paid. The Government should not, can not constitutionally, farm that great and sovereign function of all sovereign governments out to subject governments, much less to private corporations, not even banks."

To bring it close to home: suppose Farmer Jones got gold coin for all his products — corn, wheat, cotton, tobacco potatoes, hay, fruits, vegetables, eggs, poultry, milk, butter, beef, cattle, pork, hogs and other products and livestock grown and raised on his big farm and ranch, and when he bought any farm or ranch products he could CREATE NEW MONEY — just hand to the seller IOUs, on and on, for years, and never had to pay a single IOU, and he used them to buy fine clothes, fine cars, fine horses and richest of feed for them and food for himself and family, fine residences, more and more fine farms and ranches, and on finding he could buy all his neighbours' products of their farms and ranches with his IOUs, and resell them for double what he paid for them and get gold, he quit farming and ranching, rented them to tenants, moved to the city, entered politics, corrupted the Congress, hiring it to outlaw all other IOUs and make his legal tender, and soon he owned the whole nation.

You are a dairyman. You must buy or raise your cows, buy or raise your food, build barns and milk houses, hire men to tend the cows. You and they rise at 3:00 o'clock in the morning to milk them, that you may have milk to sell. But suppose you sold the cows, fired the helpers, and bought a thousand milk cans, and you could reach out and shake an empty, closed 'can and it would instantly be full of milk. How long would it take you to get rich? "The banker CREATES the BANK DEPOSITS by a flick of the pen to purchase $60,000,000,000 interest- bearing U.S.. Bonds" (in 1942), says Cong. Patman. Then why should not the dairyman CREATE MILK by a "flick of the milk pail?"

Can you now see what the authority to CREATE and CONTROL money means? Means to bankers in riches, in power? Means to the producers, workers, in poverty, in helpless servility?

Greed Grew. So Did Bonds.

The First World War put the bankers in sight of ownership of America. So they began to look around for other safe investments. They had stolen the people's farms, ranches, homes, industries, goods and tools of production. They now wanted a mortgage on their souls. The Government through its unlimited taxing power could take a man's, last dollar from, him. They decided that U.S. Bonds would give them a mortgage on the souls of men. So in 1917, hiding behind the First World War, the bankers set out to accomplish that end. The first debt limitation bill, written by bankers, passed as written, passed Congress as the first Liberty Bond Act in 1917. It authorized the issuance of $7,538,945,400 in Bonds. The following tells the story:

Authorized Sept.		1917		$7,538,945,400
Increased Apr.		1918	to	12,000,000,000
"	July	1918	to	20,000,000,000
"	Mar.	1931	to	28,000,000,000
"	May	1938	to	30,000,000,000
"	July	1939	to	45,000,000,000
"	Feb.	1941	to	65,000,000,000
"	Jan.	1958	to	280,000,000,000

Then Pearl Harbour. Limit jumped in March 28, 1941 to... $125,000,000,000. The sky was the limit. The bankers stopped the little fellows who had been pouring tiny millions into gopher holes — raking leaves in never-visited parks, lining with stones the ravines running through the bankers' large blocks sprawling over vacant portions of thousands of towns, building parks in out of the way places, killing stock and ploughing under cotton while millions were naked and hungry, sleeping on thin, knotted mattresses, — that was spending money too slow. They would never push Uncle Sam $100 billion in debt with cheap New Deal spenders.

They rounded up the Frasers, the Kaisers, the Fords, the Durants, the Du Ponts, the Hughes, the Garrsons, the Mays — the big contractors, the bigger the better, the crookeder they were the more contracts they got.

The bankers said to them through the soft-voiced High Priest of Banking, Barney Baruch, "To hell with the cost. We are in clover again. We are in war. Jobs will multiply. Money will triple. Sirs, the sky will be the limit. We will build unneeded plants, remote from raw materials. The most costly way will be most pleasing to us. We will spend $15 million on a magnesium plant in the village of Austin, Texas, which will never turn a wheel; a $60 million iron furnace in the potato fields of East Texas, and its furnace shall never glow. We will hire all the crackpots we can find to think up crazy schemes to waste money. Go, go out to spend, pad your expense accounts, never forgetting the cost-plus formula" — and the poltroon Congressmen hung on the "elder statesman" Barney Baruch's words, doing his bidding, as he ordered them again and again, as the War lingered, to raise the debt (bond) limit. And the limit was pushed to $300,000,000,000!

Look, you spineless Americans who bear the burden without trying to do something about it — look at the following figures taken from the Report of the Treasurer of the United States, issued Oct. 1, 1946, giving the highest war debt, on Feb. 28, 1946.

TOTAL: $279,764,369,348.28

(More than physical value, in 1932 dollar, of continental United States.)

Through private loans, banks had run private debt over $500 billion, and the public debt — school, municipal, county, district, state, and national — all owed to banks, amounted to more than $500 billion. So on February 28, 1946, the 141 million American people owed the 14,567 banks a $1,000 billion — a stupendous sum, $1 trillion, which fastens upon every man and woman, every boy and girl, every child a debt of *over* $7,000. (Written in 1948.)

Recalling the Panic of 1893 which bankers planned and carried out that they might through mortgage foreclosures "own three-fourths of the farms east and west of the Mississippi" as typical of their schemes to steal the farms and other real estate of the Nation, and leave "the people tenants as in England!" you will understand that it required just a few years of 20th century to complete their total rape of the Nation. So they turned to U.S. Bonds — see them grow in billions:

1917 — $1 billion; 1919 — $26 billion; 1940 — $42 billion; 1941 — $54 billion - pre-Pearl Harbor; 1946 — $276 billion; 1958 — $280 billion.

And Wars I & II did the JOB! Completed title to 171 million souls!

"BUT, STILL I DON'T BELIEVE BANKERS TRANSFER PRINCIPAL TO THEIR PROFIT ACCOUNTS," you say. Well, sir, you mean you do not want to believe that you and 171 millions of Americans would let them get away with such gigantic fraud, as Stamp branded banking. As college graduates, even with your Ph.D. degree, you have heretofore glibly and unashamedly said, "I do not

know anything about money," feeling your admission would waterproof you against being classed as a "crackpot or money nut," and now, as the whole horrible truth begins to seep into your mistreated and mistaught minds, you rush for the sand dunes so that you may stick your silly manhandled heads in the sand. You don't believe because you have been taught that bankers made all that's good possible, and you fear you might starve if you lost your master. He may be a fraud, you admit to yourself, but maybe his fraud, you reason, keeps you. Well, brother, it does — keeps you in bondage.

You say, "Of course, they take title to real estate, livestock, implements, crops and actual property they foreclose on, but admitting the banker CREATES the bank deposits he lends the borrower at the time he makes the loan, when the loan is paid the banker writes off the principal and takes credit for the interest only, which decreases the total deposits the same amount the loan increased them. He wouldn't need to keep the principal because he can create money at anytime he wants it."

Let me emphasize a fact:

Every Dollar a Banker Creates Ultimately Buys for Him a Big Dollar's Worth of Something! When a borrower pays off a note he gets his note which reduces bank's assets. To keep bank deposit books balanced he debits the borrower's account the amount of the payment, which "tends" to cancel that amount of bank deposits out, so his bank deposit books nicely balance; but bankers, as all good (?) business men do keep two sets of books and over in the little black books the bankers write down the bank deposits which were "tending" to cancel out. They are not "bank deposits": they are "undivided profits" and are out of circulation, and will remain out until stockholders meet and vote them into surplus fund (still out of circulation), or set them over in bank's building fund (still out of circulation until spent) or declare a dividend which puts them back in circulation as bank deposits subject to cheque to the personal accounts of the stockholders. They write cheques and the deposits are back in John Q. Public's hands, where they stay, being shifted from the buyer's account to the seller's account. They have served the bankers, adding the principal plus the interest less the cost of doing business to their wealth.

The bankers have lost control of them: and the only way they have of getting hold of them again is to sell their securities, principally Government Bonds. When they bought the securities they created *New Bank Deposits,* they gave seller a deposit slip and a cheque book for the bonds, but when they sold the securities, the buyer handed them his cheque which was an order instructing the banker to transfer from the bond buyer's account to the banker's black book the price of the bond, and old deposits for the second time were out of circulation and the property of the banker, but ready to return at the nod of the stockholders as before. The only way to "cancel out bank deposits" the bankers use is to "bust certain banks," and let the depositors lose, not the bankers.

"But that would be *fraud,"* you say. Yep, I say it's *fraud,* and so did Sir Josiah Stamp. Remember? So did

Jefferson, and Lincoln, and Wilson, and Roosevelt, too late. Why Jesus called them *thieves* !

But still too stiff-necked to admit that you are a slave to them because you are too lazy to think it through, or too much of a coward to stand up and face their jibes and reprisal? So you splutter, "Why, if they did that they would soon own the earth." Yep, you are right. "They do" said Sir Josiah. He also said that you could take their title to the earth away from them but let them continue to create and control credit and money and they would soon hold title again.

Remember?

Another thought: if bankers carefully cancelled out the principal of every repaid loan, what would such honesty lead them to do when they foreclosed on a farm or cattle? Would they send notice to depositors, saying in part, "Sir: We loaned your money to Joe Doak and he failed to pay it back so we had to foreclose. But due to our safe and sound blanking practices you will not lose anything. Sir, you will gain many dollars. The farm is worth three times what Doak owed us. We sold the farm for a very good price and after deducting interest and costs, we are crediting your account with $159.23, your money we loaned Joe plus your percentage of the profits." No while bankers for hundreds of years have been lying: "We lend our depositors' money," no depositor ever received a notice like that, but millions have gone to get their deposits only to find bank closed — all deposits lost.

Of course the bankers try to keep John Q. Public ignorant of their practices. Of course lazy, long-suffering, gullible John Q. Public has been told over and over and over and over for hundreds of years that the banker is the leading citizen of the community, that John Q. always before making a business deal, buy securities, or make an investment, "should see his banker." So damn fool John Q. steps, out of the way and grins when the banker passes with a "howdy, John."

Private control of credit and money has made all the peoples of the earth abject slaves of the bankers. The millions of people of India of the Bahamas, of the tropical island, of Egypt, of Palestine, aye sir, of the British Islands, have been brought under bondage by Josiah's bank, and systematically robbed, plundered, and starved.

A few years ago I was chequeing my banking information and I asked the head teacher of "banking" in one of our largest Commercial Colleges a number of questions covering the creation and control of money, and the shifting of accounts, and he looked completely astounded. He seemed to be searching my face for marks of sanity. Had a crackpot gotten into his office? I waited. I won. He took a deep breath and said, "I don't know. I was taught banking in our best schools and have been teaching banking for years. I thought I knew all the answers. Come back two weeks from today and we will discuss your questions." I had type- written the questions in the form of declarations. He pulled them out of his desk, and said : "I must answer yes to every question and these facts should be taught in every school to every student but, I would be fired if I taught them here."

"To sin by silence when they know they ought to protest makes cowards of men." — *Abraham Lincoln.*

Chapter IX

Some Further Reasons

Why Banking Must Be Abolished

Article I, Section 8: The Congress shall have power to coin (create) money, regulate the value thereof, and of foreign coin, and fix the standard of weights and measures.

Article I, Section 10: No state (then certainly no private corporation) shall ... coin (create) money; emit bills of credit; make anything but gold and silver coin a tender in payments of debts.

Certainly these three means of "regulating the value of money" have failed: (a) make all money gold and/or silver coin, (b) make gold the money standard with private corporations in control, (c) "fix prices on wages, goods, rents, and profits," as Mr. Baruch induced the Government to do in last two great World Wars.

Modern life could not be served with metallic or paper money; but it is being served by the substitution of deposits on the books of the banks to the credit of the people. This money can be used by means of a personal cheque.

Deposit money can be limited, or fixed in volume, and therefore its buying power can be made constant and fixed. Not by fixing the volume at a fixed figure, but fixing its volume at that proper ratio to the business the

Nation transacts in any given year. If you keep the ratio of money constant. The Reserve System has a board of 19 members who meet tri-weekly. They could fix this ratio so definitely that the buying power of the dollar would be constant; that is, if that were their purpose, but it is not. Their business is to make profits; not for their customers, the people of the United States, but for the stockholders, which constitute a very small percentage of the people of the United States.

That they might get more and more investment obligations, for ten years now, they have been pouring bank credit into the money stream of the Nation, making the dollar cheaper and cheaper, until today it buys on an average about one-fourth as much as it did in the 30's and early 40's.

Now their vaults are bulging with "investment obligations," and they have decided that it is time to begin foreclosing and taking title to the lands and industrial and commercial properties of the people of the United States. A few months ago these 19 kings of America met, scratched just common, ordinary chins, and used just ordinary brains, and came up with the idea that now is the time to put on the squeeze. So tight money followed, up to now just for the little man - the big boys are still building houses in blocks costing many millions, but the little fellow who had been building a house at a time, selling it, paying off the banker, then borrowing again to build again, can't get a dollar.

Remember 1929, and the years that followed, and curse yourself for not compelling Congress to take back the creation and control of money, and the Nation's credit then.

If Congress should "remember" the Constitution, and take over the creation of money, and its control, cash and clear the people's cheques, the Congress could play the role of the 19 kings, to the benefit of all. When the Treasury found the volume of money inadequate, Congress could order the Treasurer to give the Government credit in its chequeing account for that additional money the increased business of the nation required, and the ratio would remain the same. Of course they would not automatically siphon this money off when the demands of trade fell below the ratio to the volume of money, so the Congress, in its power to regulate the value of money, could "fix" prices at the status quo level.

Congress could not legally or constitutionally profit in the creation and control of money; neither could the employees of the Treasury who would man the thousands of United States Treasury Depositories, for they could not buy investment obligations, nor make loans. Their sole business (duty) would be to keep accurate accounts of the people's depository deposits, cash their cheques, and clear them exactly, almost, as cheques, are now cashed and/or cleared. The system now in use is fairly simple, but the Treasury would simplify the mechanics of money much more.

This will be developed to greater length as we give you the Constitutional Solution.

There is another emergency which may confront Congress at any time: war. If that should happen again, and we would be faced with another $250 billion war costs, the Congress would order the Treasurer to give Congress credit for the $250 billion. Since it would not draw interest, or disturb our total deposit volume, except as the Government chequed it out for goods and supplies, and services, it would make no difference if the Government never chequed it out; for as long as it remained to the Government's credit in the Treasury, it would have no effect on our money supply.

As the Government chequed against the $250 billion it would transfer these deposits from the Treasury to the people's accounts in the Depositories of the country. It would swell the volume of money; but Congress would immediately fix prices on all commodities, wages, interest, and what have you and there would be no increased costs of goods.

At the end of the war, should our increased business activity fall off, and return to normal; the Congress would take these extra billions out of circulation, as explained elsewhere, and the deposit dollars would nicely balance the dollars business required annually.

No army of "experts" would be needed to keep the Congress posted; it would be as simple as keeping Congress posted on the post office needs and activities. No smart lawyers would be needed to interpret contracts, and pile up mountains of gobbledegook, to confuse and to mislead the people.

Perhaps the most difficult proposition for the people to grasp is how bank deposits are obtained. This is so because the people have been taught that bankers lend cash, and that when they get the cash, if they do not want to have it in their possession, they "deposit the cash" in the bank, and get a deposit slip, showing that they have the cash on deposit in the bank.

This is wholly erroneous. You do not borrow cash; you borrow bank credit, and bank credit is a fictitious fund carried on the books of banks. When you borrow "bank credit" you are given a deposit slip, as stated above, which shows in the loan that bank credit was converted into bank deposits.

You must remember this; there is no relationship between volume of cash and the volume of bank deposits. This is strikingly shown on Page 25, Reserve booklet 1939, which gives total cash as of December 31, 1938, in circulation as $6,856,000,000; yet at that time the bank deposits in all of the banks of the United States amounted to hundreds of billions of dollars.

So in our discussion remember that bank deposits are readily convertible into cash, and that cash is readily convertible into bank deposits; and that loans have no bearing on cash, and cash bears no relationship to bank deposits.

Surely you get the enormity of it, the crime of it, the unconstitutionality of it. Surely you see that the bankers have created money until today it is not worth 10c. on the dollar.

There has been grave disagreement among the people of the United States on the interpretation of the Constitution of the United States of America: (a) those who contend that we should obey the letter of the Constitution; (b) those who contend that we should obey the spirit of the Constitution.

I have ever been one who believed that we must obey the letter of the Constitution, because there is no human power of mental analysis that can state that "this is the spirit of the Constitution," and give more than his interpretation of the Constitution - and there would be as many "spirits of the Constitution" as there are those expressing an opinion of the "spirit of the Constitution."

The framers knew that. They wanted to outline a specific foundation for our Government, and knowing that this could be done only in specific words, chosen because they expressed exactly what they wanted the Constitution to say to future generations. They did not use a single useless word; they expressed the purpose of the Constitution completely, clearly, in just fifty two words.

Chapter X

Some Examples Of Pyramiding Of Profits

There are six interlocking groups in the United States, which make it possible for them to continually and systematically rob the people of their wages and products. They're creatures of bankers who dominate them. They are named in order of their sinister power:

1. The 14,537 banks who have the absolute power of life and death over every human vocation, business and institution in the United States—an octopus with myriads of tentacles, with innumerable suckers fastened to every human activity;

2. Holding companies who water all public service corporation stock, dictate their practices and policies, and suck their earnings so dry that there is nothing left out of which to pay decent salaries and wages;

3. Stock and Commodity Brokers, headed by the New York Stock Exchange, Chicago Wheat Pit, and New Orleans Cotton Market, with hundreds of branches, where thousands of men and women gamble on the finances of industries and their products, while a few men manipulate the prices of every product of farm, ranch, forest, mine and factory, fixing and fluctuating the prices so that the producers in every line of human endeavour are robbed of a just price for their products;

4. Stock-issuing corporations, led by United Steel in iron, Standard Oil in petroleum, General Electric in

power and light, General Motors in automotives, Bell Telephone and Western Union in communication, and many others who dominate every industry and

5. Insurance Companies barnacled on lives and properties of the people of the Nation.

6. Oil and gas. These six groups of interlocking industries, headed, dominated by the bankers of America control and dominate every firm, business and individual of the 171 million population from the cradle to the grave, enriching a few, pauperising many many millions who have less than a bare living. In each group control narrows down to a half dozen men, and only three men dominate banking: J.P Morgan and the Rockefellers of New York and A.P. Giannini of San Francisco. And that narrows the 14,537 banks down to just three: Morgan's City National, Rockefeller's Chase National, and Giannini's Bank of America (Italy).

Let me give you a couple of examples:

A Dallas Texan, R.L. Thornton, who grew up on an Ellis county farm "where he picked a lot of cotton and a little learning," as a modest (?) one-bank banker; and a San Francisco Californian, A.P. Giannini who spent his boyhood on a produce wagon, gaining much business knowledge and little schooling, as an example of the stock-floating chain-bank bankers.

On October 24, 1916, during World War I, just before the United States entered the War I, R.L. Thornton, a penniless salesman, borrowed $20,000 and opened in an old restaurant a new Dallas bank. Twenty-seven years later, he moved his Mercantile National Bank with $184 million resources into its 30-story $5 million building ten blocks up the same street, November 15, 1943, during the crucial years of World War II, when everyone was urged to cancel improvements and to devote 100% of his time and resources to winning the War. Those $184 million resources are not all the chickens the $20,000 nest eggs hatched.

Many times the gains listed as "bank resources," went into purchase of property in the name of officers and stockholders, and in companies financed by the bank. Can you calmly ponder that accumulation of wealth in just 27 years — $20,000 into $184,000,000 goes 9,200 times original $20 thousand investment, just a bare 920,000% increase in three decades! and not want to aye, resolve to stop it? Maybe you want to be a banker. Well, how are you going to get a charter? R. L. and his crowd were busy telling us dumb Joe Doaks that we ought not to miss the wonderful "savings bond" investment — "why you just pay $18 for this bond which will be worth $25 in just ten short years." Why that is a poor man's investment, Joe. Just be reasonable and appreciative. Why, boy, that's a chance in a lifetime! a real chance to put your little money to earning money in a big way? Why, that's 70c. a year your little $18.00 will earn. Just do a little figuring, Joe. There it is. Over 3%. To be correct to four decimals, it is 3.8888% per year!

Of course Bob and his buddies were raking in just a mere 30,666% profit a year. But, my boy, they are big fellows. Why, Jodie, they rule the United States, but if you Joe, just must have $18 to run down to Lufkin to

pa's burial, and if you will get one of their good
depositors to sign a $25 note to be paid in 30 days, they
hand you the $18. Of course that is paying them
interest at the rate of 133-1/3% a year in advance!

On October 17, 1904, in a San Francisco old waterfront
saloon building. A. Giannini opened up the Bank of
Italy with $10,000 of his own money plus $140,000 his
Italian buddies put up. In one year it had $1 million in
resources and six months later it had increased to
$1,900,000.

Then the earthquake, but five years later it had reached
$11 million with six branches. Then in 1913 he bought,
400 miles away, Los Angeles Park Bank with $6 million
assets. "Buying and merging banks is easy," said
Giannini. "People don't understand that as soon as you
buy a bank you have cash and assets, and as soon as
you take over you get your money back."

He simply paid by handing each stockholder a deposit
slip which created new bank deposits. He never
touched a dollar of his $11 million assets, and after
adding the Park Bank $6 million the Bank of Italy's
assets were $17 million. By 1919, at end of World War
I, the Bank of Italy's assets had climbed to $150 million,
just a measly 100,000% profit on his original $150,000
in 15 years!

That's too slow for produce boy, Giannini "Big Bull of
the West " So he added to straight commercial banking-
financing corporations, selling his own and, other
corporation securities, and handling investments. By
1927 he had $200 million assets. His stock-selling

machinery could float $50 million to $100 million new stock issue overnight. A $100 share in 1919, after many dividends and a split up, reached a value of $1,700 in 1928. Said Giannini "I made $80 million profit for my stockholders in one year, $90 million the next." A linotype operator bought 100 shares in 1921 for $20,000, found them worth $150,000 in 1928, a 750% increase. He retired. A young bank teller found his earnings to be in 1928 $1,500,000.

Then Morgan began to sell Bank of Italy short, and the linotype operator went back to his machine and the millionaire teller took his old bank window back. Giannini fled to Italy, trying remote control; then to Austrian health resort. He resigned his American official bank connections, asked that they send him $791,000 he claimed under an old compensation agreement. They refused to pay. That so angers Giannini that he forgot his polyneuritis, and slips back to America in September, 1931, and gave battle. He got back complete control. He was 61. With New Deal largesses, followed by World War II profits, which trebled his now Bank of America assets, and in 1946, at the age of 77, Giannini the son of a poor Italian immigrant and fruit vender, stood at top of the *Biggest Bank* in the world, with its assets" $6 billion, passing its two Wall Street rivals, Morgan's City National and Rockefeller's Chase National by a hot half billion! His Bank of America today, 1945, with its 500 branches sprawling over California's 780-mile length (written in 1948 — the banks have continued to multiply) carrying 40% of all bank deposits in California and spilling over into Oregon, Washington, Idaho, Nevada and New Mexico has made Giannini not only the biggest banker in the world, but the most sinister man in the world. "Giannini has so much power," one California banking authority said, "that he could start a depression throughout the entire West simply by going conservative — that is, calling in their loans and investing in U.S. Bonds."

In 1929, just before the October 24, 1929, crash, he declared to a Senate Banking Committee, "I would make branch banking nationwide and worldwide. It is coming, gentlemen, and there is nothing you can do about it." But in less than a year, his Bank of Italy stock hit $62.50. He hurriedly drew out $2,400,000 and slipped away to Italy to be near Mussolini his personal friend, whom he admired. He was showing true banker-spirit — fight until routed, then grab all in sight and run for cover. After the war, he rushed back to make good his threat of nationwide branch banking. Now he and Morgan and Rockefeller, and branch bankers, are working together to establish worldwide banking, before the cataclysmic crash. Giannini and all other bankers *know* it's *almost on us*. If Bretton Woods worldwide banking plan goes over, it will be full 100 years of private banking crimes, because control will be so remote that the people of a nation will be helpless, and the world peoples are so diverse in thought and reaction it will be impossible to arouse them to concerted action, I fear.

Do you want this to stop? Then turn to Congressional elections. Congress is to blame for every economic crime committed in America since the first Congress, assembled in 1789. The Constitution specifically delegated to Congress the power to create and control our nation's money (Art. I, section 1), and as specifically denied the power to all others (Art. I, section 10).

We have given an example of the one-bank banker, and a chain-bank banker. Both used same methods.

The usual commercial banking and financing, securities and investments, and their big money was in the last three. There is another type — all small banks are wholly commercial, and restricted to minor loans, purchase of minor securities. If banks were restricted to straight commercial loans and minor rediscounts, their power to do injury would be greatly reduced.

But even then the fact that all of them lend credit instead of cash — that is, all of them *create new bank deposits* each time they make a loan or an investment, or buy a security, the practice of private banking would be intolerable, because (1) the creation of money through *loans* makes *debt* the *basis* of *money* when certainly *production* should be *basis* of *all money*, (2) their method of creating money keeps the volume in circulation constantly fluctuating, so that the price of everything man sells or buys is constantly fluctuating, and a most casual economic study convinces one that prices should be constant and uniform.

The proof that the volume of money and not supply of goods affects prices is found in prices of land which always skyrocket with inflation of the volume of money, and no one knows the truth and danger of that fact better than the banker. Over and over he has played the game; made money plentiful by making many loans; and with high commodity prices, men buy farms, ranches, businesses and homes at high prices, making small down-payments with the little money they have, giving many vendors lien notes for balance. The bankers generously buy your notes with new money they create, inflating volume of money still more, sending prices still higher, until their intended harvests are ripe; then they quit making loans and call in loans, taking money out of circulation. Prices drop. Farms, and homes bought on 30c. cotton, $2.00 corn, and $1.20 an hour wages, can't payout on 10c. cotton, 65c. corn, and 30c. wages. So the bankers start their harvesting machinery. And that's the third reason why private banking must go.

No group of men should be permitted to exercise such baleful power. As in 1929 Panic, thousands will hold on to their inflated shares too long and faced with poverty will suicide, while millions will suffer years of privation and want. Not so with all inner circles of banking — the stock market manipulators and their inner circles, the holding companies and their inner circles, the stock-floating corporations and their inner circles, and insurance companies and their inner circles and a few smart individuals—they are unloading their corporation stocks and bonds quietly and in small quantities, so as not to attract attention, and are buying tangible assets— farms, mines, houses, small debt-free businesses.

That started a high land-price spiral. When the rank and file discover what these inner-circle folk are doing, they will rush their holdings on the market. It will be too late for them.

A few columnists are hinting at the truth we have been shouting for years that too much money makes high prices. Below we quote one of them.

Henry Hazlitt in Newsweek

"European governments today... decree that regardless of how much they have debased (by creating too much) their currency, prices in terms of those currencies must not rise... They are united in the cry that there is a money shortage, implying that it can only be cured by further big loans from America. Our own government accepts this "dollar shortage"" explanation. Yet there are more outstanding dollars today than *ever* before. Between June of 1939 and June of 1947, total demand deposits and cash outside of banks increased from $33,360,000,000 to $108,500,000,000. This huge outpouring of dollars is the *basic cause* of the rise of prices in this period. There is more than three times as much money as before bidding for existing American goods. We, too in short, have debauched our currency. But government officials, instead of recognizing this inflation as the result of (Congress) their own (stupidity) policies (in turning over to private banks the power to create and control money), blame the businessmen. They start monopoly investigations and prosecutions which are thinly disguised attempts to put the blame for prices on business," (and keep the people from laying the blame on the bankers where it belongs). Parenthetic words are mine. The Author.

Why don't all educated men bring their combined mental powers to the task of smoking the bankers out?

Why didn't Hazlitt once mention the banker's sole responsibility for "debauching our money"? Why did the SEC, controlled by Morgan, fight so hard to keep Giannini's banks from reopening after all closed in 1933, only to have FDR and his new Deal advisers to give him the green light?

Were Roosevelt and all of his many advisors wholly unaware of the banks' blame for the 1929 Panic and the complete breakdown of our economy? If they knew, why did FDR not recommend to Congress that it outlaw private banking, restore to itself the creation and control of money, and deny all banks permission to reopen? My son, Mark Adams, who was in Washington employed by the Government from 1935 until he volunteered in 1942 for Navy service, says they erred in this as in every other instance, in feeling they could outsmart the old regimers playing ,their own game, but the Morgan-Rockefeller-Giannini-duPont cabal, the riders of the four horses of the Apocalypse, War, Famine, Pestilence and Death, made monkeys of FDR and all his Don Quixotes. Mark relates this incident:

"It was in the late thirties when best elements of the New Deal were already fighting a desperate battle against well-heeled attackers from the corporation fold. I attended a dinner over a little restaurant a few blocks from the capitol, where the Young Turks in Congress met once a week to talk over current problems. Sen. Bob La Follette talked about taxes, how to keep corporations from dodging their share of the tax burden, how to keep them from shifting the load onto the poor. A smaller group of us afterward drove out to the home of Jim LeCron, who was then Assistant

Secretary of Agriculture to Henry Wallace. We talked more about why the New Deal was failing, trying to discover where the plain, producing and serving people were being held down, what mistakes we had made, and how we might do a better job tomorrow.

There were five of us: Jim LeCron, our host; Maury Maverick of San Antonio, whom I admired for his courage and energy as the common-man's advocate in Congress; Carl Sandburg, the poet- historian and biographer of Abe Lincoln and staunch supporter of all that was good in New Deal; Bob Montgomery, economist from University of Texas, who has a rare gift for stating economic conclusions in terms of the plain people's common sense, and me, a youngster sitting in a corner and listening with both ears — and they're good ears — like a buck private who has turned up at a meeting of the Joint Chiefs of Staff. They talked of particulars for a while and the outlook on the current efforts wasn't bright.

"They then began discussion of why the good parts of the New Deal were stymied so often and the bad parts like RFC got special green lights. We knew we were losing the fight for the hard working plain common people—losing ground, foot by foot, and why? What had been the turning point?

"The administration could have done anything it wanted to in March, 1933. The people would have backed up President Roosevelt and Congress on any step they saw fit to take. The trouble seemed to be that no one in authority or close enough to be heard, seemed to know what the source of the trouble was.

What had been the New Deal's fatal mistake? Was it they saw hunger and distress and took up corporation tactics and methods and applied them in effort to succor the underprivileged, hoping to arrive at the right solution by the trial and error way?

How had greed and evil somehow preserved themselves?

"What was the fatal mistake?

"The answer was unanimous. The great mistake was made in March, 1933 — when President Roosevelt, after total crash of private banking, let them reopen as private banks again and return to the evil practices that had led to crash after crash in sickening cycles for 150 years, each move more destructive than its predecessor, resulting in the 1929-1935 Panic, leaving every American on his knees!

"I remember that. The good parts of the New Deal were failing and hard pressed in 1938 because the banks had been left in the hands of private bankers in 1933. The mobilization and production for war got under way with painful slowness in 1941 because the control of credit and money was left in the hands of greedy vicious private bankers in 1933.

Too late, it was all too clear! Wherever we found greed and oppression on the march, found people suffering, when we dug into the background we found the evils and oppressions stemming from bankers every time. Banks had been granted by Congress absolute control of credit and money, a grant of power over civilization which ultimately controlled all — damned near all! And as long as private greed-groups hold that power, as long as three men like Giannini, Morgan and Rockefeller can dominate a nation of 141 million people, (written *in* 1948) the plain working people will be kept on their knees and painful poverty and defeat will stalk 135 million of us. That was the considered opinion of the best informed and the most courageous men I know. That's a summation of what they had learned through bitter defeats while fighting in the people's cause. And I remembered — just in case.

"It is a lesson for all to remember. If ever again the common people rise up as in 1932, and set about a righting conditions" as they tried to do in 1933, the first step is for Congress to resume its own constitutional power to create and control our money, and to rescind all banking laws.

If a power to 'lift UP or cast DOWN' all the people is to be held by any group, that group must be the people's own duly chosen Congressmen, which was so wisely couched in the Constitution by our founding fathers.

"That was the sum of a sincere and informed post mortem on the New Deal — the clearest I ever heard, and I remember it. And you would do well to remember it, too. And to ponder it! And to act," concluded Mark Adams.

Personal History of a Bank

The bank picture and a story appeared in *Dallas News,* October 13, 1946. R.L. Thornton, president of bank, was born in a half dugout, graduated from the Corn, Cotton and Mule University. He opened a Private bank on $20,000 borrowed capital, at 704 Main Street, Dallas, in 1916. He took in $12,000 deposits the first day. Thirty years later his bank, The National Mercantile Bank & Trust Company, moved into its own 30-story building, which was built during the war when the rest of us could not build a home, at a cost of $5 million. He had climbed 30 stories in thirty years, his assets climbed from $20,000 to $184,000,000 — a gain of 920,000 percent, or an annual growth of 30,666 percent profit a year. And that did not include the millions drained off by means of bond sales, stock sales, dividends, etc., which went into ranches, oilfields, beautiful homes, which did not register as "assets of the bank", and other millions went to pay the expenses of their "in-the-family white trash", who have beaten trails to the four corners of the earth Yellowstone Park, tables at Monte Carlo gondolas in Venice, pyramids of Egypt, hot sands of Miami — all places where international white trash swarm and lounge with billions of American "credit dollars" steaming from their fingers.

That story is typical. That is a niche in the "House Banking Built," which Josiah Stamp said OUGHT to be torn down.

The man and woman who live without turning their hands to honest toil, who live by their wits, are creatures of banking, their lives of non-toil made possible by these bankers "creating" debt dollars which would buy the products of those who must toil to live.

CHAPTER XI

MORE OF THE STEPS IN

THE CREATION OF MONEY

First, there is the Reserve, authorities power to write a cheque against no funds.

Page 85 of Reserve Booklet: "Federal Reserve Bank credit ... does not consist of funds that the Reserve authorities "get" somewhere in order to lend, but constitute funds that they are empowered to create. The process of creation is one of giving the promises of the Federal Reserve Bank — in the form of Federal Reserve Notes and Reserve deposits — in exchange for the promises made by others to the Federal Reserve Banks, the reason for the exchange being that the Federal Reserve Banks' promises are recognized BY LAW as having a particular monetary utility not possessed by the promises of individuals or of private institutions."

That simply means that the Federal Reserve authorities can write a cheque against no funds or give the sellers of securities to the Reserve Banks deposit credits on their books. These securities are (a) U.S. Bonds, (b) Corporation stocks, or (c) investment obligations, which the member banks may sell (or deposit with them) — and the member banks get; credit to their reserve funds. If the Reserve authorities should pay for the securities (promises of others to pay) with Federal Reserve notes, instead of just giving the seller deposit credits on its books to the seller, it would mean nothing, because the Bureau of Engraving and Printing (the Treasury) prints reserve notes for Reserve Banks at a cost of only 30 cents a $1,000. To follow that course would be both perfectly silly and useless; for the seller of the investment obligations would have no use for the cash, he would just deposit the money in the bank, receive deposit credit against which he could write cheques.

The Reserve Banks are now very careful to say, "We buy U.S. Bonds and pay for them with Reserve notes." Bankers are fighting desperately to hide the fact, that, in reality, they are lending no funds; but create funds every time the Reserve authorities buy investment obligations, or make a loan, and every time any commercial bank buys investment obligations, or makes a loan. Just as Congress, by law, empowered the Reserve authorities to write a cheque against no funds; the Reserve Act empowers commercial banks, who are member banks — and there are some 8,000 (total 14,537) other State banks and trust companies who do business as branches or under trusteeship of member banks) to write a cheque against no funds.

A congressman wrote me that he used to think that when the Reserve Banks, which are the fiscal agents of the Government (keeping its deposits and clearing the Government's cheques paid to customers for materials and services) bought U.S. Bonds, that the Reserve Banks just gave the Government credit in its deposit account for the bonds; but now he has learned that "Instead money is created in the form of Federal Reserve notes taken from the Treasury's Bureau of

Engraving and Printing, and used to buy United States Government Bonds." He has been brain washed.

The Congressman did say this: "... when Government bonds are bought for the 12 Federal Reserve banks, the capital stock and surplus of the banks is not used for this purpose, and funds of the Reserve banks are not used for this purpose, and the deposits of member banks are not used for this purpose."

The Congressman is wool-gathered in the assertions that the Reserve banks use Reserve notes (greenbacks in daily circulation) to pay the Government for the bonds. He is not wool-gathered in his statement that they do not use capital, surplus or bank deposits for banks do not, never did lend their capital, their surplus or their depositors' deposits.

But let's note how silly the Congressman's assertion that the Reserve authorities get from the Government Reserve (free) notes, and then hand them back to the Government in payment for the U.S. Bonds. The Government prints these bonds for the Reserve Banks at a cost of only 30 cents a $1,000 and the Treasury keeps them in storage, just like a printer would keep a customer's letterheads in storage, doling them out to the customer as he called for them. The Government took blank paper, and printed some gobbledegook on both sides and presto it is money. The paper is 21/2" by 6" and it may be a $1 bill, a $5 bill, a $10 bill, a $20 bill, or a $50 bill on up. It is a fiat of a private corporation, made legal tender by printing "The United States of America " promising to pay the bearer Five Dollars, and in very small 4 point type, legend for all debts, public and private and is redeemable in lawful money at the United States Treasury, or at any Federal Reserve bank."

The Government has printed for the Reserve Banks $27,371,374,795, which was blank paper, but when printed in bills, the above value was affixed on them. So the below-cost cost of the printing amounted to $8,181,412.20. How would you like to hand Uncle Sam say $30 and he would hand you $100,000? Well that is what he does for the poor, impoverished, full of-pity bankers.

Now about that money (Federal Reserve notes) the Treasury hands the Reserve banks that they may hand it back to the Government in payment for the bonds. Of course that would be all right, because the Government would hand it right back to the bankers and say, "Just give me deposits for the money — can't use cash in my business; always pay with cheque."

But you see the bankers can say that "we pay cash for U.S. Bonds; and they could say that Uncle Sam printed that "cash" for just 30 cents, a $1,000 (but they don't); so it didn't cost us anything." Then they could add: "Why, the old geezer just took deposit credit for the 30 cents, and the deposit credits just cost the trouble of writing them on the books, and clearing the old geezer's cheques — yep, they don't grow dumber than that Old Uncle Sam." They only whisper that behind closed doors.

Let's, borrow $1,000 from your local bank. You sign the note, put on top of it chattels worth

$3,000, then pay credit insurance for a $1,000 — all for the banker. (If you don't pay, the Insurance company will, finally) — and you hand all (note, mortgage, insurance policy) to the banker, and the banker will count out to you very carefully, $1,000 in Reserve notes, which cost the bank nothing; and you will hand them right back to him, and say, "I prefer deposits; taking that much money out would be dangerous; some one might rob me — any way, I always pay with cheque because that gives me a good receipt to show I have paid my bills."

Silly way to lend deposits, isn't it? But a Congressman said that that is the way the Government borrows money from the Reserve Banks. The truth of the matter is that 99 percent of all money borrowed, and paid to customers for investment obligations, is deposits (on the books of banks) transferable by cheque from [begin page 132] buyer to seller. And the Reserve booklet says: Page 39, "The aggregate deposits in the banking system as a whole (are) funds lent by banks or paid by banks for securities."

Let's get back to that summation I was going to make of the processes of the creation of money (bank deposits).

Second, the Reserve authorities give a corporation its cheque (remember against no funds) for its stock, $10,000,000 worth.

The corporation deposits this cheque in its Austin bank, and the bank gives it deposit credits, $10,000,000. These are new deposits, increasing the total deposits

$10,000,000. The Austin bank sends the cheque to its Reserve Bank in San Antonio and the San Antonio Reserve Bank gives the Austin bank credit in its reserve fund, $10,000,000.

Third, The Austin bank now has $10,000,000 added to its, reserves. It can lend five times the $10 million, which would be $50 million, and when its customers borrowed the whole bank credit, or apart of it, and the bankers used the balance to buy investment obligations, and they perhaps would, the Austin bank's deposits would be increased $50 million.

That's the whole story. That is all there is to the creation of money, the customers' deposits. First, a Reserve cheque is written; Second, it is deposited in a bank; Third, it clears through the bank's Reserve Bank, and the Reserve Bank gives Austin $10 million reserve credits; Fourth, the Austin Bank lends five times its reserve fund, or buys investment obligations with it, creating in this way $50 million additional bank deposits to the credit of customers of the bank. When these notes are paid off, and they resell or collect the investment obligations they buy, then the $50 million will be their cash assets, growing out of the fact that a corporation deposited a Reserve cheque with them. Can you find in the whole chain where the Austin Bank paid one thin dime for its reserves, its bank credit, its $50 billion in notes, etc.?

Now I have written many words in an effort to let you see how bankers have euchered the Government out of the Nation's credit — taken over the creation of money and the control of credit. How the Government must borrow from the private corporations. The story is astounding in its volume and implications.

At the end of World War II the Government had issued $250 billion in bonds. At the beginning of the war, the previous bonded indebtedness was a mere $46 billion.

Mr. Patman had tried to get Congress in 1943 to adopt a resolution which would make all bonds owned by banks non-interest bearing; and said at the time that "we are entering a war that will probably cost us $300 billion." Then the bonded debt of the United States increased as a result of World War II, over $250 billion, falling $50 billion short of Mr. Patman's fears. The Reserve authorities bought the entire $250 billion, and then sold part of the $250 billion to persons and corporations. They prefer this for two reasons:

First, it lets them say that the people let the Government have the money to fight the war; Second, they got the bonds as a free gift from the Nation, so when they sold them to the people, as many of them as they did sell, they converted the bonds into deposits to the bank's credit. That's why they fought Mr. Patman's desire to make bonds into two classes: (a) those to sell to the people directly; (b) the rest to sell to the bankers directly. Had this been done the bankers would have been deprived of one of their richest revenue sources; for as often as they sell a bond (and they could not sell a bond if it did not bear interest) they add the price to their deposits; and as often as they buy a bond back, they give new deposits for the bonds; thus they get them back from the people just as they got them from the Government, *free.*

The Reserve Act gave the Reserve Banks arbitrary and absolute control of credit, enabling them to increase bank loans or restrict the flow to a trickle. Their chief method is to increase or decrease the ratio between a member bank's reserves, and its deposits. But often they do this by ordering banks to raise interest rates and refuse to make loans.

When we have good times, they open the floodgates, bankers begin to lend bank credit frantically, and a gullible people begin to borrow, and spend like drunken sailors. Employment increases, goods flowing from industries become a torrent, and riding merrily along on a "debt dollar" the people coast up and down life's highways exhilarated by speed and "wealth." But, when the Reserve board decides they have enough of such human joy, good eating, cavorting hither and yon, they can arbitrarily "dry up" the banking funds, and borrowers walk away without deposit slips and a cheque book. Industries slow down, men are laid off, cash becomes hard to get, and men with holes in the soles of their unpolished shoes, tramp the streets, besiege employment offices, looking for work... and vacations with pay become "periods" without work; and hunger gnaws at the vitals of men, women and children; and the smiles of good times become frowns, dazed looks, and melancholia becomes an epidemic.

How the Squeeze Is Put On

We are now in the midst of one of these criminal squeezes. Word went out to bankers, "No more loans, except to the elect; raise the interest rate; make credit too expensive to use, hard to get."

We are today helplessly watching bloodless corporations set the tables for another catastrophe which will make the 1929-1934 debacle, in retrospect, just a holiday.

These are the men who sit tri-weekly in the offices of the Board of Governors of the Federal Reserve System, "grapple with the problem: whether to pump more money into citizens' pockets, or siphon it out; give us inflation, or hair-curling depression... They are the seven members of the Federal Reserve System's governing board, and the presidents of the twelve Federal Reserve Banks, scattered about the country." Those words were quoted from the Saturday Evening Post, July 20th, 1957 issue. It does not name the 19 (only 19 men from our 171 million people) men who compose this group. It does give a photograph of them in action; and graciously prints the picture and gives the name of the President of the Board of Governors of the Reserve System: "William McChesney Martin, Jr." and he looks exactly like any small town banker, no smarter and perhaps no dumber.

These nineteen just ordinary men, swelled into national and international largeness by their positions, hold good times and bad times for all of us, in their hands.

The terrible fact is: Profits, their profits, is both their god and patron saint, and this obsession blinds them to every human value, shuts from their view the 171 million of us who must eat or go hungry at their will. If banks, small, individual banks, fail through their "stringency" or lack of credit, imposed by these 19 men, in the language of their progenitors, "they ought to fail they are not needed." If businessmen go broke, and farmers lose all, in the language of their progenitors, "They ought to lose they are too rich and too independent." If you remind them that this act will cause wide-spread hunger, the children of the workers will have no bread, they will, as smugly as Queen Catherine, say, "Then let them eat cake."

Nothing, nothing, nothing concerns them but profits. And, as they did in 1837, 1873, 1893, 1907 and 1929-1934, they will not hesitate to wreck the country, rob millions of their property, their life's savings, that they may take title to billions of dollars worth of property, because the debtors can't pay their mortgages.

They are the visible forms of Private Corporations, a "bloodless person," a soulless person, a conscienceless person, a cruel, thieving person, nerveless, eyeless, deaf; never hears the cries of hungry children, nor sees the sad, hopeless, full-of-despair eyes of the millions of bread winners walking the streets begging for bread.

Yet, you learn all of this, then say, "But we can not trust Congress, our elected men and women, the 531 of them, who are under oath to do justice to every human being in the Nation, and whom you choose to represent you?"

How absurd. You had rather be ruled by kings whom you had no part in their annointing, 19 of them, than to trust your Congressmen. Yet you know, if the Congressmen do you an injustice, you can hire another man to represent you; but whatever evil these 19 may do there is nothing you or the President can do about it.

Only Congress can do something about it. The Constitution of the United States says they must do something about it; for it says that Congress shall have "power to coin (create) money, regulate the value thereof."

How the Depository System Would Function

The depository system would eliminate all the fictitious "funds" you find shifting about from bank to bank, from Reserve account to Reserve account. The keeping of the people's deposit credits, cashing and clearing cheques, would be reduced to simple bookkeeping, deposit- keeping. It matters not in which depository the cheque was presented for deposit, there would be just the simple crediting deposit account of the receiver of the cheque, and the debiting of the deposit account of the giver of the cheque. There would be no clearing houses nor "central depository" through which cheques drawn on one depository and deposited in another would have to clear. There would be no "funds" shifting from one depository to another-only figures representing deposits would increase in one depository and decrease in another, dollar for dollar. Figures on the books, plus the cash out of the depositories, would be the total and complete representation of our volume of money.

Cash in the vaults of the Treasury or in the depositories would never be reckoned as a part of the total volume of money only the cash in the hands of the people would be a part of the total money supply there might be a trillion dollars in total minted coins and printed bills, while the total money supply might never be over

$500 billion, yet that would mean nothing, because as long as the cash remained in vaults of the Treasury and the depositories, it would be dead.

There would be no shifting of cash from one depository to another to "cash cheques". If a depository ran short of cash to hand out to its depositors, the Treasury would supply it whatever additional amount needed; and should a depository pile up too much cash in its vaults, it would just let it lie there subject to the orders of the Treasury. No depository would keep books against any other depository. It would not be concerned where deposits from its books went, or from which depository deposits came. It would simply total each night, total deposits on its books, and that would be that.

I have said elsewhere that the change over from the banking system to the depository system would not injure any small businessman. I should explain that it would not if he was using an honest dollar, not a stock-market or phoney dollar.

Texas is plastered with several layers of "insurance company's, policies." Thousands of these are doing business with the most spurious stocks as their "fund" securing the policy holders. Within the last 15 months Texas has shocked the Nation with its infamous U.S. Guaranty, and Trust company, which had dealt in stock, pyramided spurious assets, only to crash... the president did a very worthy thing, he shot a hole through his head. Then there came the hydra- headed BenJack Cage's finagling, and he lost to the Unions and thousands of stock holders in his many companies millions of dollars, and so powerful are these crooks that he came back from Brazil only after two Texas district attorneys promised him practical immunity from punishment, and at this time he is in Texas having a Roman holiday with grand juries and House and Senate "investigation committees." He has made monkeys of all of them — and the press hangs on his "mighty" words.

When Congress takes over the creation of money and the regulating its value, the keeping of the people's deposit credits, cashing and clearing their cheques, this thing can not happen.

You will not witness what is happening all over the United States, a "squeeze" placed on the "little man" by 19 sinister men who meet tri-weekly with the power to shut off money from those whom they wish to destroy — and definitely now they propose to utterly wipe out the little fellow as an independent operator. Mass production lies have so clouded the people's minds that now they are saying "Get a job with some big corporation, and behave yourself, and your future security is assured." I see here in Austin the big contractor going right on with his many-million-dollared development projects, while the little fellow is searching for a job with the *big* fellows.

This is an apt side light. We commiserate the Russian people under the stateism that directs everything and compels everyone to labour at some task. We forget that the masses under the Tzar were vassals of princes who owned the lands and the villages and cities. These vassals worked for the barest necessities of life-stones on the great estates. We are headed back to that situation. This cheap, phoney dollar bankers are flooding the nation with is being used to buy up the land, and thousands of families are being driven from the land, into the slums of cities, to be a burden on the Government.

The 19 Reserve men (they claim legal authority) symbols of the Russian regime, hold the power of life and death over us all. We use different terms to describe our activities, but they are parallel with Russian power and disregard of the rights of the masses. The power of these men, the destructive influence of the phoney dollar, will be swept away, and only the honest, eager-to- serve-mankind associations of men will be able to survive, and they shall prosper because the Congress will see that no legitimate enterprise, *essential to the well-being of the Nation, will suffer for lack of funds.*

Spurious insurance companies, faking trust companies, innumerable 'trust estates, and the gambling in stock markets, wheat pits, cotton markets, the casinos — these barnacles on our ship of state will be roughly scraped off that the old "Constitution" may again sail grandly and proudly in the sea of nations.

CHAPTER XII

CREDITALISM VS CAPITALISM

The world has been cursed over 250 years by *Creditalism* parading under the banner of *Capitalism*. The people of every nation who toil and produce every human want, the masses, *have come to hate the term Capitalism,* and justly so because credit has been parading as Capital. And the users of the people's own credit have not only robbed them of the use of it in their own defence, but have created against the people a $250 billion debt during World War II. Creditalism parading as Capitalism has won the hatred of the masses of the entire world because wherever it goes it robs the masses of the products of their toil, takes from them title to their lands, either ruthlessly kills them or forces them to toil for them as peons for peons' wages and builds palaces and skyscrapers — and call it the "great works of Capitalism."

The peoples of Europe take America's food and turn from us to Russia not because they love or want Communism, but because they hate our brand of Capitalism more and want it less. The people, the producing masses of the United States, even the whole world are turning against Creditalism as we know it and feel it today.

There are two sources of Capital — that is, of money:

1.   The production of goods, which is itself an act of creation. The amount saved becomes true capital

which is stored or investment capital. That is true private capital, and the person who created it has a perfect social right to use it as he pleases. It is honest capital. It represents wealth which he has created. It will always be limited to that portion man saves out of his production of goods for all of us; therefore it could never become dangerous. A nation financed on earned capital would be a democratic nation because no individual or group could become strong enough to dominate or destroy individuals or other groups. A person or group needing more capital than he or they had, would borrow earned (existing) money from others, and no new money would be created and added to existing volume to inflate and cheapen it. This sort of economy truly would be sound, beneficent Capitalism.

2. The creation of bank deposits by simply crediting the bank customer's account when "the bank buys from him any security" — his own note and mortgage, deed of trust, or government or corporation bonds, stocks or shares, or any other commercial paper. The bank gives nothing of value. The act is called a loan, but you can't lend nothing. But the act creates by a "flick of a pen, out of thin air," bank deposits which are transferable from buyer to seller, hence it performs the primary and chief function of money, a medium of exchange. Bankers call it bank credit, but that is untrue. It's the people's credit, made attractive on the faith of the people's own Government. It is Creditalism and not Capitalism. It gives bankers absolute control over all production, all transportation, all communication, all education — all industry, all trade and commerce; and, in effect, title not only to the real wealth of the Nation, but title to its earning power.

Will You Now Agree That What Might Have Been Must Come To Pass?

Well, fellow citizen, you have read that frank sketch of the most sordid set of human creatures ever spawned by selfish greed. You will find my simple, constitutional remedy equitable and sound.

There was just one zeal dominating me as I sketched the "Crime of Banking", and outlined the "Remedy", and that was America's greatest contribution to the tenets of organized government - "Equal Rights for All; Special Privileges for None."

I believe that the Declaration of Independence of 1776, and that the Constitution of the United States of 1787, are the greatest economic documents ever penned by men that they, sketched the "Crime of Special Privileges," and charted the course of "Equal Rights to All," so clearly, so succinctly, that no one can fail to understand them. Smart men, among them were smart lawyers - men who knew the exact meaning of every word they used-wrote those immortal documents and their desire, which they consummated, was to write so simply that all minds could understand them. They knew that any document which required a lawyer's interpretation was dangerous.

I believe that in spite of the fact that Congress has failed to obey all of the simple injunctions of the Constitution, and permitted selfish men of greed to wangle unconstitutional laws out of them, there is no other nation's government so worthy of its citizen's love and devotion. With all of our official shortcomings and corporation abuses, none of it is due to our form of government, nor to its foundation, nor to its objectives. We Americans love our form of government so much that we will suffer grave injustices in our laws, hoping that Congress will right them in the American orderly way. I believe Congress will set the House of Money in order soon.

I believe that Congress will redress the grave wrong the Supreme Court committed when it declared corporations to be persons, and set the House of Corporation in order.

They are now awaiting a mandate from the people. Let's briefly look at *What Might Have Been,* if Congress had obeyed the Constitution and coined or provided the money of the nation. First. There would be no huge corporations dominating industry, but there would be thousands of small industries scattered throughout the nation giving the people a finer and a more personal service.

Second. There would be few monster cities, if any; but there would be thousands of small cities hovering around widely dispersed small prosperous industries.

Third. There would be fewer "fine" residences and country "estates", but there would be millions more pretty little cottages with children romping on ample lawns.

Fourth. There would be fewer country clubs, big cars yachts and seaside resorts, but there would have been thousands more small cars and small family cabins down by lake and stream, where millions of families of workers could spend restful weekends.

Fifth. The skyline would not soar in isolated blobs, but millions more one-two-and three-story buildings would fresco the horizons of millions of contented people who owned not only their homes and business houses, but their souls, too.

Finally there would not be a $250,000,000,000 national war debt hanging over us.

What Might Have Been If —

Now, let's see what would have happened if our plan had been in operation:

1. Congress would have frozen all prices, all wages, all salaries, all invoices, all deposits, and every human being, physically and mentally able to render any form of service, would have been automatically conscripted into service, each left at his task, or sent where he could best serve. Each would be paid a living wage with food, lodging, other expenses, if sent from home, plus care of dependents. All materials and supplies, would be requisitioned, and all sites for camps.

All deposit credits would become a revolving fund, subject to Government check for expenses. The $100 billion plus on deposit would have been ample funds because it would have poured out in a steady stream as the Government wrote cheques for materials, supplies, labour and services, and rushed right back when the person took it to bank for cash or deposit.

All materials and supplies bought would be at the pre-war fixed prices. All service charges, all wages, all salaries-all price structures would remain on pre-war bases. All non-essential businesses and activities would be suspended. All private money lending would be suspended. Every person would be employed and directed by the Government. No profit. No new private business. No loafing. No shirking. No strikes. No get-rich fellows. Just one big family working and fighting, with but a single thought — to win the war, and — WIN IT FOR KEEPS - and win it quickly!

Remember: under my plan there would be no BANKERS, so the money situation would be simple. Depositories would be kept busy shifting accounts back and forth between the people and the Government. It would be *just* like a $10 cheque Brown writes White for corn. White endorses cheque and hands it to Black for oats. Black endorses it and hands it to Green for a shoat, Green endorses it and hands it to Redd for hens. Redd endorses it and hands it to Smith in payment of debt he owes Smith. Smith buys a Stetson from Goldstein, and he rushes down to the depository and deposits the cheque. The depository debits Brown's account $10 and credits Goldstein's account $10. Probably neither White, Black, Green nor Smith had a deposit account. Certainly it was Brown's deposit account giving value to the cheque, and there was only one $10 involved, but it paid for $50 worth of stuff and settled a $10 debt between Brown's writing the cheque and Goldstein's depositing it, it had done $60 worth of business — ends up $10 on deposits. No one was injured least of all Brown, owner of the $10 deposits. His cheque transferred the $10 deposits to White, and each re-transferred the deposits until Goldstein asked for final transfer from Brown to him. Time element meant nothing. A day or 365 days would have resulted in same endorsements, same stuff bought with final transfer of deposits.

That is exactly what the Government should have done, used the existing deposits over and over until the war ended. Each would have been paid for his time and his goods. There would have been a continuous flow of deposits from depository to person, from person to person, and from, person to depository, the Government acting exactly as the pump that sucks up the water out of the pool, forcing it through nozzles. The water falls right back to be sucked up again, over and over. The Brown $10 did as much business as, six cheques if each cheque had been redeposited by first recipients.

The Government having the control and the use of its own credit, there would have been no bonds engraved, and no new deposits created under total manpower conscription. The Government would have operated all businesses — farms, factories, mines, forests, retailing, wholesaling, communication and transportation, so all cheques issued would ultimately return to the Government for redeposit. There would not have been any bond sales, and stars would have had better jobs than osculating pot-bellied bankers at bonds sales. Not only all able-bodied men and women, but property, all money and every business would have gone to war —

sure, it would have been a total war, and we would not have had the rank abuse of rank that some would get more pay — private to general, janitor to superintendent would have been well fed and clothed, and paid a small stipend for fun and recreation.

Oh! You wouldn't like that? I didn't think you would. Neither did those privates who slithered on bellies in mud to reach the foxhole only to be mangled by a bomb. If a boy 18 may be compelled to face that, why should you escape?

Yep; that's right. There'd be no war, if every person had to serve without profit or hope of reward other than victory. Cut out blatant flag-waving, battle-dodging, profit-stealing patriots, and you'll cut out war?

2. At the close of the war, the re-adjustment would have been an easy, a painless, and an inexpensive task. All persons would have returned to their pre-war stations. Everyone's business would have been restored to him as it was before the war — same invoice, same location, farm, forest or whatever the business was before the war: same stock, implements, tools or equivalent values of each. Every pre-war employed person would return to his pre-war job and pre-war pay, picking up threads of life where he left them when the war took over. No one would be any richer or poorer, unless he had saved some of his war pay.

Every depositor would have his pere-war account unfrozen and added to such deposits as he saved from his war pay.

A short while ago the vice-president of a Dallas bank said, "Another depression is ahead, and when it comes it will be a honey." He must have felt that his dumb slaves would do nothing about it. Remember what the President of the American Bankers Association said to his fellows assembled in Baltimore, in 1931:

"We the men assembled in this hall, we men who *control* the economic destiny of this nation, knew in 1927 this *terrible* depression was coming, and *we did nothing about it*."

And he could have quoted the American Bankers as having said, in a circular to all bankers, in 1891: "We authorize our loan agents in the Western States to loan funds on good real estate to fall due on September 1, 1894, and at no time thereafter. And on and after that date we will not renew our loans under any consideration, but on September 1, 1894, *We Will Demand Our Money*. We will foreclose and become Mortgagees in possession. We can in this way take two-thirds of the farms west of the Mississippi, and thousands of them east of the great Mississippi as well, at our own price... We may as well own three-fourths of the farms of the West and the East and the money of the Nation. Then farmers will become *Tenants as in England!*"

Chapter XIII

Cash is Not a Part of Our Money Supply

All discussions of money stress the importance of the volume of cash, giving it an undue influence on the money supply... even today we hold to the fallacy that silver and gold have a great influence on the money supply. In its latest edition of the Reserve book, "The Reserve System — Its Purposes and Functions," the writers urge the importance of great floods of cash flowing at certain times, and assert that the money supply consists of cash and bank deposits. To make the cash a part of the money supply is absurd, because that is like saying that you have two men working all of the time, when as a matter of fact, they never work at the same time.

When one is asleep, the other is working. If man was like money, tireless, one man working continuously would accomplish the same thing, you might see the fact better. This can be verified with electric engines. They work on endlessly and never tire. It would be foolish to buy two engines to do the work one can easily do.

Depository deposits and cash are both used in buying and selling, but never at the same time. You either cheque the cash out, or use a cheque book to pay seller. When you take cash out of the bank, say $50, your deposits will be lowered $50, which will lower total volume of deposits $50, but when you or the seller returns the $50, the deposits will be brought back to normal volume.

Cash is exactly like the personal cheque. When in the hands of the buyer, it is active, real value. Take your own bank account. You cannot have both the amount in cash and on deposit at the same time. Say you have $500 deposits in the bank. When you write a cheque and draw out $75 in cash, your account is debited $75, and your new account is $425.

In trying to establish the fact that you must add cash to deposits to arrive at the total money supply, the Reserve book says: "When a person has $10 in his pocket and $100 in the bank, he is in a position to spend $110. These two kinds of money represent his cash resources." The writer forgot to say that he or some other person had to write a cheque against his deposits and draw the $10 out; and when the $10 cash reached his hands, his deposits were $10 less.

The very circulation statement (of cash) disproves that cash is apart of our money supply. Circulation Statement of United States Money, May 31, 1957, gives total cash supply at $55,095,658,926, and out of the Treasury and in circulation, only $35,191,638,399; then they whittle that down again, having "in circulation," that is in all of the 12 Reserve Banks and some 14,537 commercial banks" $30,636,348,266. So you see that $24,259,310,640 of the total never leaves the Treasury... and to all intents and purposes is dead.

There is an interesting observation we may make here: while gold certificates are outlawed, and cannot circulate, and get in Joe Doe's hands, this statement shows that the Treasury has printed for the Reserve Banks $21,964,687,524 Federal Reserve Gold Certificates.

Then this same circulation statement shows under kinds of money gold, which, too has been outlawed as circulating money, total $22,620,251,821. If you add this column, and we must admit that every item listed is "money" (when in circulation), you find that the *grand* total is $79,457,122,476. That indicates that we have just lying around, not active, dead, $48,620,774,190, about $18 billion more than the banks find use for in the circulation of money. It is interesting to note that in 1934, on the insistence of the Reserve folks that we go off the gold standard, take gold coin and gold certificates out of circulation; then raise the price of gold from $20.67 an ounce to $35 an ounce; then buy up all of the gold in sight, the Treasury, not the Reserve authorities paying for it; that now we find that those Reserve boys' Midas hands have gripped Uncle Sam's throat, compelling him to print at no cash outlay to them over $21 billion Federal Reserve Gold Certificates) which gives them title to the gold Uncle Sam bought, and spends millions guarding as if it were a sacred cow. And it is a sacred cow to scheming bankers. Why print the gold certificates if they cannot circulate? They can't even reach a commercial bank; they lie in the treasury, another police risk, and doing the people not one bit of good. It is merely some of that gobbledegook bankers peddle. If they base bank deposits on Corporation stock, why do they want Gold Certificates?

Well, from absurdity to absurdity you travel if you follow the mysterious trail the bankers blaze for you when they dare to talk.

Since either a cheque or cash must be used by the buyer in paying for a purchase, then they are identical, and not by any stretch of the imagination can be made separate monetary funds. The only volume of money is reflected, or would be if all deposits were reported in the bank statements, in total deposits (all deposits) in all the banks of the nation. These deposits are used in buying and selling, or should be, and whether the seller takes your cheque, or whether you cheque the cash out and hand it to him, is immaterial. The fact remains, as admitted by the Reserve book, that someone must write a cheque and present it to his bank, before cash can leave the bank. And when you leave the bank with $10 you just drew out, your deposits are debited $10.

I bought an American Express Company's $10 travellers cheque, a few days ago that I might photograph it for use in this story. It cost me 50 cents, or I had to add 50 cents to a Reserve $10 note, to get this American Express Company's $10 travellers cheque. So the cheque seems to be better money than Reserve notes. For the same reason I bought an express money order, and a postal money order, again paying a high tariff for the exchange.

Then if we must add to the bank deposits the volume of cash in the treasury and the banks arrive at a total volume of money; we should as the total of all companies' travellers and money orders, also total p.o. money orders, to arrive at a grand total, for these are just as good money as Reserve notes or silver certificates, as for that matter. The same as with personal with personal checks ... good when signed and presented to seller.

You never saw a report of postage stamps in the post offices, total amount, and volume, etc. The postage stamps have no value until taken out, and Uncle Sam is paid for them, not when he sends them to the post-offices.

Had you ever thought that banks do not lend their capital, nor surplus, nor undivided profits, nor the cash in their vaults, and that they never report their deposit credits? That when you read a bank statement appearing in your papers, that it tells little or nothing about the true business of banking? A teller in a bank brought to my office once, the bank statement which the Government requires must be printed periodically, and when he handed it to me, he remarked: "I don't see why those statements are printed. Nobody understands them, and they don't reveal half the banks do.

So my dear fellow victims, it matters not how many billions of dollars in cash may be minted and printed, the only "cash" available to you is the amount of your deposits. You ordinarily will pay with a cheque, but when you do not, you chequed the money out of the bank, and the check just did it work before you made the purchases.

I have gone to this length to prove to you that the cash should not be added to the volume of deposits in all banks, to arrive at the volume of money in the Nation.

There is no relationship between volume of cash and volume of deposits. Cash is provided for your convenience as cheques are provided, that you may trade your deposits for goods. Your cheque is not good until you sign it, the cash is not good until you draw it out of the bank. As with postage stamps, the amount or volume minted and printed is of no importance, beyond having an ample supply or volume to meet the demands of the people.

Cash (coin and bills) is nothing in the world but tokens, having one advantage over personal cheques, and that is it will be received without question by all sellers, and does not have to be signed. Cash is a general cheque, and like all cheques, of no value until in your possession.

If Congress would compel all banks to report all funds (deposits and cash) on their books, additional width would have to be given the deposit totals, for it would run into the trillions of dollars.

The cry the bankers make is that their system is the only way a flexible and fluid money may be provided in times of business high activities. When the Government takes over the keeping of the people's deposit credits, cashes and clears their cheques, Congress will see that the volume of Depository Credits is ample to meet the highest business demands; and when business is slack, the surplus deposits, like cash in the vaults, will just lie there and slumber until some phase of the moon sets the people about new and frenzied enterprises, as since World War II, but under the Depository System there will not be high and low business activities-normal, steady, purposeful progress at all times. The gamblers, create cycles of low and high activity; and bankers are gamblers!

Honest, legitimate enterprises, and industries, and businesses will never lack funds under the Depository system; for that will be the constant responsibility of Congress, to see that the volume of deposits is adequate at all times; and there will be no "pumping in and siphoning off" as now practiced by banks. There will be no indebtedness requiring siphoning money off that debt may be foreclosed. When people are rushing ahead building, developing, advancing as in the early 50's, the Congress would not grow alarmed about the luxuries the people were enjoying; it would not, as the 19 Reserve men did in 1955, stop the pumps, which had been pumping money into the people's pockets; and turn to the exhaust pumps and begin frantically siphoning (pumping) the money out.

Don't let them frighten you by saying that there will be no money for advancement, improvement if we stop them. They now plead for lower income taxes that they may "save funds" for expansion and development — never using them for expansion, always, issuing more corporation stock! If they are only using profits for expansion, the banks serve them no purpose. As we need more money, Congress will order the Treasury to give the Government deposit credits for the needed additional amount. This will be chequed out for expenses of the Government, and flow right into the deposits of the people. It would be a creative act, but an act only Congress can Constitutionally perform, and it would benefit every person in the Nation, because it would save taxes, as the money would first pay Government costs.

That is what we do under the Reserve System, add new deposits to the credit of the Government; but the bankers do a lot more: they require Uncle Sam to issue bonds to amount of new deposits, say $100 billion, which the people must pay taxes to pay the interest on these bonds and still owe the bonds. So under the Depository system, there would be no bonds, no debt to private corporations, no taxes to pay interest.

And remember this: under the Depository system, new deposits would be created at rare intervals, and then by an act of the Congress; but under the present Reserve system, every time the commercial, or Reserve Banks, make a loan or buy an investment obligation, they create the face of the loan or purchase in *new* deposits, which find their way into the total volume of all bank deposits. That sum is, so stupendous that I don't think the banks will try to amass them, total them.. or maybe that is what they have done, and when the 19 men who meet tri-weekly in New York to puzzle over the banking business, saw that stupendous total, it scared the wits out of them, and they at once stopped the pumps pumping deposits into the deposit totals, and hastily started to siphon it out of the hands of the average man.

They did this in 1955, and gradually economic paralysis is extending over the entire economic body. Building is off, manufacturers are finding their goods mounting with no one to buy, men are now walking the streets looking for a job... men are always anxious to work; and only a cold-blooded corporation would sit and squeeze money out of their pockets by making jobs scarce because money is shut off.

Yes, the Depository system will dry up this flood of new deposits pouring in daily; but the Congress would see to it that the body would always have adequate blood in its arteries. And inasmuch as both cash in the vaults and deposits are dormant, and have no influence on the deposits and cash circulating, we arrive at the conclusion that only the active money affects industry, business, our economy.

There might be too much deposits in the volume on the books of the Depositories, but there would never be too little to meet an legitimate enterprises of the Nation. I have just received through the mails an expensively engraved formal announcement of the "formal opening of their newest H.E.B. Food Store." There is an engraved picture of this "store," which covers several thousand feet of floor space; and there have been paved thousands of feet of parking space for customers' cars. The whole covers approximately four blocks.

There is an old H.E.B. Food Store a few blocks down the same street, vacant now, which has been adequately serving such customers as needed its service; but another "big food" man who has climbed from rags to riches via the grocery basket, had opened a grocery store in a new trade centre, and was no doubt taking a lot of trade from the old H.E.B. store, so the H.E.B. company just dug into its stock till and came up with some $500,000 new deposits to build this "emporium," that it might hit the less big fellow a wallop on the head.

Until recent years, even great cities like London and New York, got along nicely with the little corner grocery; but now in this town of 160,000 people, we have many, many great food stores, many, many trade centres; and we understand a fellow is now developing a $30 million trade centre, and it will have its great "food emporium." There are now many littler Du Ponts, who have their fingers in both industry and banking, and the easy way of getting deposits through the issuing of new stock, and selling them to the Reserve authorities, is expanding every line of trade and commerce beyond a wholesome limit. Not only was there no need for these great stores, but in creating them, thousands of small grocery-men have been driven out of business.

That is what cheap, unlimited new deposits is doing for us. As said elsewhere in this book — too much forms tumours, and death follows unless expert surgery is performed.

First we had the one-car family; then the two-car family; now the many-car family, one for each child, and one for each parent; but now we have expanded housing to the two-family house status. Our just abdicated governor has several — one in the Valley, one in Woodville, his birthtown, and a mansion here in Austin!

Our U.S. Senator Johnson, as a life-time public servant, has gone from rags to millions; our last two governors have gone from rags to millions, and they have been in public service all their majority lives. They could not have gotten these riches if deposit credits were not mountainous, and the transferring of them was not so easy with no detection possible. I think of two statesmen before every loan created new deposits: Clay and Webster. They too had been in public service all of their majority lives. One day Webster said to Clay, "Would you please go on my note for $500 at the bank?" And Clay replied, "Certainly; but, by the way, I need $500 dollars; my grocery bill is pas It due; so you sign my note and I'll sign yours, and both of us can ease our financial embarrassments."

Ex-president Martin Van Buren spent his declining years in New York, and he was a familiar person, with grocery basket on his arm, as he did the grocery buying for himself and the former First Lady of the Nation. And be sure to get this: I am not advocating poverty, I'm advocating honesty!

The hundreds of thousands of new cottages, residences, palaces which have sprung up like mushrooms over the entire Nation, were an built on the credit dollar. They could have been built at a fourth of the cost under the Depository system, with an honest dollar. Had money been available in ample volume, there would not be trillions in notes, vendors lien notes, investment obligations in the hands of a few thousand people.

Whatever you enjoy on credit, is not wealth; it is a tumour which will utterly and ultimately destroy our Nation. These silly "housing projects" will disappear, and Congress will have sense and guts enough to enact a law which will set a minimum standard for all houses to be rented; and for a family of two to build a fourteen-room "ranch monstrosity" to wander about in, when a little five room cottage would afford them all the housing they need, will be outlawed. You say you have a right to build any size or sort of house you want. Well, you may find that a priority could be employed, which would not let you take scarce materials and labour to build for you unneeded space when others are in shanties and shacks.

The Government would not be, under the Depository system, interested in profits for itself. It would have no mountain of investment obligations to collect. There would be no incentive to slow down production, and foreclose. Its whole effort would be to keep the normal activities of the people moving smoothly, unobstructed. There is as great demand for goods, aye greater, now than in 1954, when the sky, was the limit in employment and business activities. As long as people will work, and produce and consume, nothing should interfere with their progress. No 19 men should have the "legal" power to pump money into the bloodstream, or pump it out.

Don't feel that we just couldn't do without the banks. If you will recall the hundreds of billions of dollars we have paid and must continue to pay the bankers for the privilege of using the Nation's, our own credit, and know that all these costs have been not only unnecessary, but as clean a steal from the people, as the stealing of your horse, never to recover him, you will not want to continue the banking system.

All this prosperity (?) you see about you is not the making of bankers. It all grows out of the fact that people want to work, they want to produce, they want to consume; they want cars, TV s, gadgets, good clothes, and homes, and days off to relax. Instead of the bankers giving us all this, they have charged us 300 percent on every dollar they have permitted us to use. Go over again the cost of the World War II. $250 billion bonds given them gratis. We have paid them in the last 10 years $100 billion in interest; and they have an added free $1,250 billion funds they can lend or use to buy any investment obligation. Add the $250 billion U.S. Bonds, and they got $1500 billion gratis out of the war. The people got only the $250 billion deposits given the Government for the bonds. The bankers got six times as much. This alone should make you swear that private corporations shall not coin our money and then do nothing about regulating its value. The banker does not plan, or promote industry. He sits there and compels you to pour your earnings and your savings into his pockets.

Contractors, big contractors who are developing housing projects running into the millions, after the little fellow has been choked off by the bankers, are finding it profitable to sell $20,000 residences on the right side of the river, for as low as $500 down payment, and take long- stretched-out instalment notes for the balance. They prefer this method, because the banks take their "investment obligations" off of their hands (of course at a big discount, but then they have a big profit), and they have to pay income only on the $500!

The Keeper Becomes the Landlord

A few days ago my neighbour, the operator of a one chair barber shop, living in one of the "small-down-payment" cottages valued at $7500, finagled his small investment in the cottage down here where the melting pot is going on with a might, and "bought" a $20,000 home in the Hills, where only the rich are supposed to live. He must pay all costs of this mansion, pay the taxes (which are not so high a rate as his cottage, because the rich have a way of getting low renditions), pay for the repainting and repairs of the mansion (for the "articles of sale" provide that he must keep it painted and in good repair or the lien holders can do the work, and assess the costs against the "owner," which become a first note to be paid, and you pay or they foreclose, and you lose your little investment; and on top of that he must pay the premium on the $20,000 credit insurance policy the same articles of a sale demand, and they can pay the premium themselves, and present the bill to the "owner of the $20,000 mansion," and it too becomes a first note to be paid.

Who owns that mansion? Certainly not the barber; perhaps his entire cash investment was not over $500. Then why the sale? The owners of that "mansion" did not want, nor desire the cash. Had they taken the cash, that pesky, snooping robber Uncle Sam, would have come in some fine morning and said, "I don't find where you reported the sale of that $20,000 mansion

for cash!" But the dumb very dumb Uncle Sam, lets the *big* boys write the income rules, so they don't have to report the "investment obligations," only the cash they receive; yet the "investment obligations" are lying in the bankers' vaults, and are monetary values just as much as are the deposit credits (cash) in the banks.

What the owners were looking for was a caretaker, a keeper in whose hands they could leave their valuable property; and instead of paying the caretaker for his services, they not only made him pay costs of upkeep, including replacing busted gas pipes, etc., but they made him pay interest (rent to stay there). Not only that, he had to pay the taxes for the owner, and keep it insured at his own cost with the credit insurance (also fire, storm, hail, and what-have-you insurance added); so that should he fail to pay the loan, or should the property be destroyed by fire, they could just take *over* the lot, and the insurance companies would have to pay the difference between what the "owner" owed and the value of the lot.

Now that is not just an isolated case. Hundreds of billions of just such "monetary" values exist. Are we a home-owning Nation? Has home-ownership increased in last 10 years, during this building boom? No for a man does not own his home until the last note is paid; and if you could see the figures, you would find that the note holders' title is flawless, and that the home owners' investment in cash is infinitesimally small compared to the volume of investment obligations the bankers hold. They do hold them in most part, because these "home boys" — these fellows whom we grew up with, and who we thought were just common fellows like ourselves — were developing acres of residential property- $6,000,000, $20 million, $30 million projects

— on borrowed "capital" which they got from the banks.

Uncle Sam Becomes the Underwriter

Well, during the late 20's boom, bankers got a belly full of "little" investments, the selling of houses to little folks. The crash left them with too many of these notes un-collectable, and the boys just moved out and there was no recourse worth taking. So following World War II, after finding Uncle Sam the biggest sap in Christendom, and that his Congressmen would go along with anything the bankers asked for, the bankers decided deeds of trust and first mortgage notes were not good enough; so they went to Uncle Sam (Barney did again — he is now 88, and seems good for 88 more years) and said, "We must not forget that these veterans have faced shot and shell, placed *our* flag atop of a mountain in Iwo Jima and their buddies died on many battlefields, so we can't be too good to them; they came back with families, they must have houses to live in; *we,* 'our Government,' should finance those houses."

Well, that is not all Barney said. He said, of course the Government hasn't money, revenues, enough to pay the costs; "and we feel that it would be unfair to ask the people to pay interest on more Government Bonds, and, too we have about all of them we can store; so in the goodness of our great bankers' hearts, they are willing to finance these homes, if you will just endorse the costs."

Well, Congress, again, said the bankers say they wanted to give the people something, and let's let them do it; so legislation passed, and it was called "Veterans Home Loan Act," and that set the people to saying, "The Government is financing the Veterans' homes; so a veteran can buy it for less down payment, get a lower interest rate, and a longer time to pay for the house." And veterans fell for it like a ton of brick. And the cautious father or neighbour said, "But, Joe, you are promising more for the house than the carpenter would build it for; that's why you get it at less interest costs - they have already added the interest, enough at least."

And Joe said, "Well, I can live in it until rents are cheaper than instalments on the house, then I will move out; I am buying it and moving in because the monthly instalments are much less than the rent I pay. I am paying $80 a month for a house not as good as the one I am "buying" and my monthly instalments are only $60."

And John, who was classed as F, but who worked hard, aided the war effort just as essentially at home as Joe did on Iwo Jima had no part in it.

Well, the father told the son, "But you can't get loose that easy. You *move* out, and the Bankers will sue *you* not Uncle Sam, and get judgment, covering unpaid instalments, plus interest to the day the court renders judgment, plus costs of court, lawyers' fees., etc., and of course you can't pay it; but that judgment may lie there on the records of the court for 100 years. Should you in the future become prosperous, the holders of the judgment could enter and possess your property, cash or goods. Of course, in the meantime, Uncle Sam will have paid off; but you are stuck for life, or until you payoff, too."

But Joe, in the interval between his 13th birthday to now, had lost confidence in the "old man's" advice and judgment, so he said, "Well, I'll take a chance."

So of the billions against "veterans' homes" are in reality obligations of the Government, but the Government would get no benefits, any more than an endorser would get should you default, and the banker collect from the friend who endorsed your note, or perhaps, signed with you.

If I could (and Uncle Sam could) get access to all bank books, all records of instalments, all financial facts, I would come up with the answer; and I would by actual figures show that in actual deeds or instalment obligations against all real estate, all industry, all transportation, all business the bankers of the United States could buy the United States many times over with their "wealth." And that "owners" own very little.

CHAPTER XIV

CONGRESS MUST REGULATE

THE VALUE OF MONEY

Now that we have dealt with Congress' responsibility of "coining money," we must now take up that more difficult task of "regulating" the value of money.

1. After Congress got full report from the Treasury, giving total deposits to the credit of the people (and the Government), and after getting from other agencies of the Government information which would lead them to a knowledge of the total business transacted in the United States in current year, the Congress would then "regulate the value of a dollar" in terms of the work it had to do. No other factors would enter; for the sole purpose and duty of money is to serve as a medium of exchange between buyer and seller, and to serve as a measure of the surplus products the people produce in anyone year.

Of course that would divide our deposits into two categories: (a) demand deposits used in buying and selling goods and/or services, and (b) time deposits, or deposits to be loaned. However, the total would be treated as a whole, because the making of loans would keep the time deposits active, not in the names of the owners of these deposits, but in the accounts of the borrowers of money.

Suppose that the Congress found that, after all monetary deposit credits of the people had been totalled, there would be on deposit to the credit of the people $700 billion, but it required only $350 billion to meet the demands of business annually. Then Congress would order the Treasurer to instruct the Depositories throughout the Nation to rewrite all deposit balances, giving each depositor credit for just half of his former balance. For example, should you have $300 to your credit on the books of the Depository, the bookkeeper would strike out the $300, and write $150. This would not cost you one penny because it would be like swapping 300 half dollars for 150 dollars. Your new $150 deposits would buy just as much in the markets of the Nation as your $300 did before the adjustment. Price tags would be rewritten at half the former figures.

This would give us a sound, stable dollar. It would continue to buy the same amount of any commodity every day. If it bought four pounds of coffee in 1957, it would buy four pounds of coffee in 1997. This would be accomplished by the Congress keeping the total deposits equal to the total cost of carrying on business as the years passed. They would do this by adding deposits as often as the total demands of business was greater than total deposits. They would add these deposits, by having the Treasurer give the Government deposits in the amount of the extra deposits needed. This would be the only creative act of Congress. When it gave the Government deposit credit for, say $10 billion, that would increase the total deposits $10 billion which would have been a creative act, for no goods, chattels, or wealth would have been involved; but when the Government chequed the $10; billion out to pay for services and goods, the $10 billion would be added to the people's deposits, becoming a part of the permanent volume of deposits, money.

As production and business increased, the Congress would in this way keep pace with deposit credits. That is a true valuing of the dollar, and gives us the soundest, most fluid dollar the world will have ever seen. Fluctuating prices would disappear; there would be no feverish writing and rewriting price tags. There would be no furniture dealer writing a price tag for $249 and hanging it on a suite of furniture; then drawing a red line in the same act through the $249, and writing "our sales price" at $129.

All commodities that did not readjust to the new dollar value, would be placed under a ceiling by Congress. There would not be allowed any speculators in the commodity markets of the world, buying up commodities, then refusing to let the people have them except through a dole which would keep the prices high.

2. There are other monetary values which are never listed among deposits, transferable by cheque. These are investment obligations, simple notes, vendors lien notes, first mortgage notes, deeds of trusts, corporation stocks, etc. These do influence the money market, and the value of a dollar just as much as too much money. Not by creating new deposits as now; but through the watering of their values; as when a company sells $100 million more shares than it needs to finance its business. Or when contractors price a house that actually cost $5,000, at $10,000, or may be $15,000.

Those notes are watered, just as corporations water stock. Land values that jumped from $10,000 a lot, to $100,000, are watered just as much as the corporation watered its stock.

When the re-adjustment day, the "judgment day" rolls around, and the Congress "squeezes the water" out of all investment obligations; this will bring the price of them down in "parity" with the sound dollar that must pay the note, the mortgage off. The gathering in of investment obligations during their pumping money into the stream, then siphoning it out, making it impossible for the mortgagors to pay, has long been a prime activity of banks. Foreclosures followed, because the note maker could not pay, and more property was transferred from the people's ownership to the banker's wealth.

As with the people's deposit balances, the Congress would have all investment obligations altered (by law) writing the principal figures at half their original volume.

Your lot that you say is worth $100,000 now, would be re-valued at $50,000; and so on down the line ... prices in most cases would voluntarily drop, but in those instances where they would not, Congress would set a ceiling price over them.

There should be only two dealers between the manufacturers or producers of goods: (a) the wholesaler, who would buy the goods, and store them in great storehouses for distribution to the retailers, for resale; (b) the retailers who would buy them only for resale. There would be no stock markets, stock exchanges, wheat pits, cotton markets, where men and women with phoney money would gamble on the guess whether the price went up or down. A few men in Chicago New York, New Orleans and a few other cities, could not then manipulate the markets exactly as the dealer manipulates the roulette wheel.

As a boy on my father's East Texas farm, we planted cotton with the cotton market at 10¢ or 12¢ a pound. When we harvested the crop in the fall, and sold it, we got as low as 4¢ a pound for strict middling cotton, picked by hand, as free of trash as careful picking could keep it.

Many of us can remember the Krugers, Lawsons, Hills, Goulds, of the yesteryear, and the Youngs of today, who manipulated the stock markets "making" millions in the steal.

With the sound dollar that the Congress can give us, and having cut out all phoney money, reducing money lenders to the lending of existing deposits, the Congress will not have to outlaw these gambling devices; for that is what they are, just as much as all of the gaming devices "legalized" at Las Vegas. They could never have *been* established, without the phoney dollar; and with the death of the phoney dollars, the bankers' pen and ink dollars, there will be laid by the phoney dollar's corpse, the corpses of the "stock market," the wheat and cotton pits and casinos.

he land speculator will go along with his buddies. Boom and busts will pass into limbo of unneeded and forgotten things.

Then truly, in the words of Sir Josiah Stamp, this, will be "a happier and a better world to live in."

The Value of a Dollar Is What It Will Buy

Fixing the value of the dollar will effect every transaction between man and man; and the strong will not be able to tread down the weak — the big club of the Nation will be there to strike him down if he tries it.

I can sense your saying "Oh, no; you couldn't trust Congressmen. They wouldn't know anything about banking, as you have shown, and bankers would use them as they use them now... and besides all politicians are crooked." And let me reply: "There are a hundred crooked business men behind every crooked politician" and then add, "What could the crooked business man get out of Congress if it could not buy investment obligations, indulge in stockmarket gambling, neither buy nor sell merchandise? Corporation stock? What special privilege could Congress grant corporations who were engaged only in the manufacturing of goods for the people? If Congress could not lend money, what would Congress have that the business man would want other than police protection along with all other enterprises, and the people? Too there would be no bankers. Only deposit lenders.

Too had you rather trust 19 men over whom you have no control appointed for 14 years; tools of private corporations who are interested in only one thing, profits for their private corporations (including the banks); who will not hesitate to take even the shirt off your back, and you have no recourse; who sit tri-weekly in Washington (not as a government agency, but as private banking corporation officials to pump more money into your pockets or siphon it out, just as their whims drive them, than trust 531 Congressmen — 96 Senators, and 435 Members of the House — whom you elect (all Congressmen every two years., and a third of the Senators every two years, giving you a chance to clean out the old and return all new Congressmen, which would give us 467 Congressmen, say in 1960, fresh from the people?) They would obey the people's wishes IF the people would stand behind them and demand that they do so as the corporations now stand behind the Congressmen and compel them to do their bidding. Take crooked businessmen from behind Congressmen and they will not be crooked Congressmen. If Congress vote against the people's welfare, if they are crooked, it is because corporations stand closer to Congressmen than the people do.

Why the upsurge of Congress in the 30s for the people rather than for the corporations, in the main, it seemed? Because the hungry people and impoverished small business men, became angry and shouted such a manifesto (Roosevelt was chosen repeatedly by the hungry and the impoverished) that all sorts of laws were ground through Congress, for the benefit of the masses. The halycion days for the masses were here, but while the people rejoiced in their saviour (Roosevelt, and a Congress who took his suggestions almost to the letter), the corporations were busy in the back ground tightening up their controls of the Nation's money and credit. And now we are in the beginning of another holocaust of dollars, all lost by the people to the bankers' private profits.

The fact that the Constitution *couches* in the same paragraph with the coining of money, the "fix the standard of weights and measures," proves conclusively that they had in mind that the value of money should be measured by commodities; therefore, when Congress establishes the right ratio between money and goods, business turnover, then it shall have "regulated the value thereof."

CHAPTER XV

THE CONSTITUTIONAL SOLUTION

The Federal Reserve System banks, with all of their faults have rendered the people two *very* essential services. First, they have created the Nation's money; Second, they have loaned money. There is a third *service* which the Constitution imposed on Congress: "regulate the value of money." If the bankers have *ever* tried to regulate the value of money they have utterly failed.

A Congressman Without Faith

Congressman Patman, speaking before the House, August 22, 1957, said:

"The Constitution is very plain that Congress shall have all power over money, but, obviously, Congress cannot administer that power. So Congress has delegated it to the Federal Reserve System, which is all right if properly administered. I would not offer any suggestion that would lead to the repeal of a substantial part of the Reserve Act, except one. That is to have the Government and Government officials carry out this important function of regulating the value of money; in other words, to determine the supply of money, the cost of money ... there is not enough interest in it... yet it is the most important subject that the members of Congress have to deal with."

He had just said that "obviously, Congress can not administer the power of 'Coining money, regulating the value thereof.'" Yet, he insists that Congress must administer the power to regulate the value of money. And that is the most difficult thing to do with money, "regulate the value thereof."

If Congress can grapple with the most elusive and the most difficult task before the Reserve Banks, the regulating of the value of money; then the "coining (creation)" of money would be just a minor problem. Bookkeepers could do that!

The coining and regulating the value of money are responsibilities of Congress, delegated to Congress, and the Constitution nowhere gives them the authority to re-delegate that power. Those are the two most important functions of the Government, the creation of money, and the regulating the value thereof; and they are public services, which no private corporation could possibly render fairly, because profits would lead them to abuse the power.

The other service the banks have been rendering, the lending of money, is not a public service, but a private right.

Article I, Section 10; The Congress shall have power... to coin money, regulate the value thereof, and of foreign coin, and fix the standard of weights and measures.

There it is in black and white.

Amendment X: "The powers not delegated to the United States by the Constitution... are reserved to... the people"; therefore Congress has no right to invade the lending of money, for that is a private right, reserved to the people.

While the Constitution gave "Congress the power to borrow money on the credit of the United States," it nowhere gave the Congress the power to lend money. The founding fathers never dreamed that the United States would lend money. They empowered Congress to collect taxes, duties, imposts and excises to pay the debts of the Nation and to pay the expenses of the Government. Therefore, they could not contemplate the Government ever lending money — it would never have any money to lend, because all the money the Government would ever have would be taxes paid in by the people; and the Constitution specifically says that "The Congress shall have the power to lay and collect taxes... to pay the debts, and pay the expenses of the Government. So where would the Government get the money to lend?

They never dreamed of Congress lending the Nation's Credit. They never thought of the credit of the Nation as being something to lend. They thought of the credit of the Nation as being the security it had to justify lenders to lend money to the Government. Had they understood the modern mechanics of money as refined by the banking system, they would not have used the word *coin,* but would have used the word *provide.*

How the Transition Should Be Made

Therefore, the Congress should provide the Nation its money, and regulate the value of money; but it should not lend money. And conversely, the Banks should lend money and not provide it. The two functions of creation and control of money should be restored to Congress; and the lending of money should be the private right of private persons.

To accomplish the returning of these powers to Congress, the Congress should take the following steps:

It should enact the United States Depository law; which should provide:

1. That the Depository System would be an agency of the Government, under the supervision of the Treasury of the United States.
2. It should establish Depositories in every community in the Nation, convenient to the people, as post offices are provided.
3. It should provide that the whole duties of the United States Depositories would be (a) to keep the people's deposit accounts; (b) to cash their cheques; (c) to accept their cash and cheques for deposit and, (d) provide an ample supply of cash register change; (e) to supply depositors with cheque books, very similar to Travellers Cheques.
4. It should provide that the depositories could neither lend nor borrow money; that they could not buy or sell investment obligations; therefore there would be no need for loan experts, bond experts, stock experts; just the simple routine of keeping the

people's deposit accounts, cashing and clearing their cheques — bookkeeping would require only the services of clerks, tellers, bookkeepers.

5. It should provide for the leasing of one-story buildings at no higher rental than commercial rentals, for the work would be very similar to the running of the post offices, construct vaults, install equipment for handling the people's deposits.

6. It should have minted ample quantities of coins, and an ample supply of Treasury notes, bills, should be engraved. Each depository should then be supplied with ample cash to supply the depositors with pocket and cash register change.

7. It should provide for the employment of a Secretary of each Depository, and such clerical help as needed, as the post offices are manned.

8. It should provide, after these preparations had been made, that on a certain date, all persons, firms, and institutions, other than banking and related corporations, would turn over to the closest Depository, all cash in their possession for deposit with the Depositories. Then the Depository would let each draw out at once, the new currency (coins and bills), in sufficient quantity for pocket and cash register change or as much as each wanted.

9. On the following day, all banks, trust companies, and other financial institutions that carried the people's deposits would deliver all cash to the depositories, but they would not be given deposit for the cash, and their deposit books to the nearest Depository that Depositories might transfer the people's deposit accounts to the books of the Depositories.

10. On the following day, all persons, firms and institutions, and corporations, other than banks and related financial institutions, would deliver to the Depositories all U.S. Bonds in their possession, and the Depositories would give each deposit credits for the principal and accrued interest on each bond — then burn the bonds.

11. On the following day, banks and all financial institutions would take their bonds to the Depositories, and surrender them to the Depositories; but the Depositories would not give them deposit credits for the bonds, unless it was shown that they had bought them from private persons without using new deposits, — and burn them.

12. It should outlaw all deposits and cash not surrendered on day designated.

13. All currency and coin surrendered would be destroyed that is, the bills would be burned, and the silver, nickel and copper coin would be sold as metal. It would have been replaced with Depository currency.

14. It should limit cash withdrawals to just pocket and cash register change.

15. It should declare the deposits of the people money transferable by cheque.

16. It should make personal cheques legal tender for all debt, both public and private.

17. It should provide that the forging of a personal cheque, the writing a cheque against insufficient or no funds a felony, punishable as counterfeiting.

18. It should have no clearing houses; no intermediate station through which cheques would pass when drawn on a Depository other than the receiver of

the cheque's Depository; but each cheque, when deposited in a Depository other than the giver's account, and sent directly to the giver's Depository, where it would be debited against the account of the giver of the cheque.

19. It should outlaw all other monetary funds, such as reserve funds, bank funds, bank credit, reserve credit (all are fictitious funds), etc., and declare the total Deposits the only monetary funds-the Nation's money.

20. It should ascertain the volume of money required to carry the Nation's business for one year; then adjust existing Depository deposit totals on that basis. If, for example, it required $350 billion to carry on the Nation's business one year; but the Depository deposits total is $700 billion; 'then the Congress would order the Treasurer to instruct each Depository to cross out the Deposit Balance of each depositor, and write a new balance. If the depositor's balance were $400, the new balance would be $200. This would not cost the depositor a penny, because the commodity prices would be marked down automatically 50 percent, and his $200 would buy as much as his $400 would before the readjustment.

In as much as all investment obligations are as truly monetary values as are deposits, it would be manifestly unfair to cut the people's deposit in half, and make no adjustment of the investment obligations; so Congress would by legislation devalue all investment obligations 50 percent.

Then the giver of the note would not have to pay a phoney value note with sound dollars.

This has been a trick of bankers for years: fill their vaults with investment obligations — your notes, mortgages, etc., then cause a money stringency which would send the volume of dollars to the bottom of the pit, making your dollar an exceedingly valuable thing, and very difficult to get; then demand payment of this "inflated debt (investment obligation)" with the hard-to-get sound dollar. This alone should forever condemn private banking, which enables them to fill the bloodstream of industry, business and commerce with hundreds of billions of phoney, counterfeit dollars, then squeeze these phoney dollars out, and demand pay in the 100-cent dollar.

It would be like my filling the pockets of all my neighbours with my "worthless IOUs" then compelling em to pay off the notes I got for my IOUs with gold dollars.

It is like lending a wheat grower $5,000 when wheat selling for $2.00 a bushel, and compelling him to pay the $5,000 when wheat is selling for $1.00 a bushel. When money fluctuates investment obligations should fluctuate in lock-step with it. Of course that would compel Congress to "fix the ceiling over and a floor under prices, wages, rents, and all goods for sale."

21. Require all persons, firms, and corporations — savings, and Loan corporations, Trust corporations

— keep their cash and deposits in the Depositories of the United States.

22. Since the creation of the Nation's money, fixing its value, keeping the people's deposits "cashing and clearing their cheques" is the most important service Congress can render the people all expenses of the Depositories shall be paid out of the Government's general revenues. No service charge would be made. No money orders would be written. A depositor would mail his cheque to any other community in the Nation in payment of a monetary obligation at a cost of only 3 cents. The free flow of deposits in the stream of cheques is absolutely necessary that our trade and commerce may be active, unhampered, unimpeded. A dollar must move to any point in the United States, and pay a dollar obligation.

How to Handle Foreign Exchange

23. The Congress, would provide a separate department of the Treasury through which all foreign exchange would be handled, preventing outside money coming in and flooding our money supply, except under express, orders of Congress. It would, with other nations, arrange exchange ratios, and otherwise keep a close watch on our foreign and domestic money.

24. In as much as every capital investment, under the erroneous, practice of "the flag follows men and money," in a foreign country, as well as all loans, involving the Government, no investment in a foreign country or a loan could be made by any citizen or corporation to a foreign citizen, except by

special permit granted by Congress after careful investigation by its Foreign Finance Commission, with like permit from the Government or Nation where investment, or loan is to be made. And should foreign investors seek to invest in the United States industries, the same procedure in reverse would have to be followed. It would be less costly to take these precautionary steps than it would be to send the Marines to collect debt — provided that no investment or loan to a foreign Nation would involve the credit of the United States — all foreign loans and investment would be wholly at the risk of the lenders and investors. All expenses of the FFC would be paid by lenders and investors.

25. Congress should provide a neutralizing step to offset the transfer of home deposits to foreign countries, so that foreign loans and investments would not reduce our volume of home deposits. This could be done by Congress selling the lenders and investors international exchange for their domestic deposits, which the Treasurer would deposit to the credit of the Government. The Government would cheque these deposits out to the people in payment for services and goods; so it would flow right back into the Depositories. On payment of the loan, or the return of any foreign investment in the form of international exchange, the Government would buy the exchange and pay for it out of revenues, which would offset the original exchange sold. All outgoing and incoming deposits would tend to neutralize each other.

26. The Congress would in co-operation with other nations create and set up an international exchange

Depository to be used in all international payments, etc.

27. After the United States Depository System had been set up, after all monetary funds had been transferred to the Depository books, the Congress would repeal all banking laws, and outlaw the use of the word bank, or the use of terms indicating that the nation was interested in any corporation, or private business-such as "U.S.," "United States)" or "Federal."

28. In the same act of repealing all banking laws, the Congress would enact lending laws, which would govern all money lending.

Some Explanatory Thoughts

Now let's explain many of these provisions of the Law which Congress shall enact in creating the United States Depository System, in obedience to the *must* of the Constitution.

First. There will be no interruption of the flow of money; for the Depositories will be open, operating, with vaults full of currency of the new series-coin and bills. The day that the customer brings in his cash, the opening day of the Depositories, he will deposit his old cash, and get new cash in lieu of it. The next day, the deposit books of the banks, trust companies, all institutions that keep the people's deposits on their books, will be in the Depositories, and depositors will be able to cash their cheques at the Depositories, or make deposits, as usual and in the same manner as when going to banks. Except that you will go into buildings very similar to post office buildings, and get new money, a new form of cheques, the normal course of your life will not be affected.

You might go into a "store building" re-equipped for the use of a Depository, as you go into a "store building" in small towns, or suburban sub-station post-offices, but your Depository would be as important as any other Depository, and render you the same service any other Depository would render. All Depositories would be on same basis — no small depository in even cities — all would be directly under the Treasury.

You would see no long line of desks with "important-looking" men, with a stenographer sitting near by to write dictation, prepare loan agreements, etc. There would be no "private office" where the "President" worked his game, or where the "Stock Experts" advised you to buy this or that bond or stock. There would be no U.S. Bond window, nor money order window. There would be only a "deposit window, or windows," where you would walk up and draw out money, or deposit cash and/or cheques; and another window where you would get your Cheque Books. There would be no five million dollar structure to fill you with awe; there would be no imposing guards to impress you that our business is very important. There would be just "our sort of folks" — clerks, tellers, bookkeepers to wait on you. You would feel so much at home. And every time you saw the words on windows, on front of building, "United States Depository," and on your currency and cheques "The Treasury of the United States," and remembered that no post office had ever failed, that the United States is, or would be, the soundest institution on earth, there would never again be in your mind a fear that "this Depository may fail, and then I will lose all my money." Complete confidence in the United States Depositories would quiet your fears, comfort your soul, and calm your nerves.

There would be nothing going on in that building but (a) cashing cheques, or receiving them for deposit; (b) your getting your cheque books; (c) and busy people debiting and crediting the accounts of the depositors would pervade these buildings.

If you wanted to send money to a distant community you would not go buy an Express Money order, or a post office money order, you would just put your own Treasury cheque in a envelop, address it, and place a three-cent stamp on it, and mail it. Your Depository cheque would be as good as a Nation could make it, as safe as a money order could be; for every cheque you wrote would be "legal tender" money.

✳F35·400·108✳

Signature of Drawer of Check   Signature of Secretary of Depository

THE TREASURY OF THE UNITED STATES OF AMERICA

When properly signed legal tender for all debts both public and private.

Date_____ 19____

Pay to the order of _____ $_____

_____ DOLLARS

Secretary of Treasury   Drawer of check

A Suggestive Treasury-Personal Check

The Bureau of Engraving and Printing in Washington would print all Depository Cheques. They would be blank cheques, similar to an American Express Company cheque. The cheque would be the same size and design as that chosen for United States Treasury Certificates, with only the capitol building at Washington as background.

The top half of the Treasury cheque would be very similarly worded to the above cheque. In the left corner the wording "when countersigned below with this signature." In right corner would be the serial number as above — each depository would have a key number, so that wherever a cheque turned up, its home depository would be easily ascertained.

At top left would be line for signature of cheque holder as on the above cheque, and date line on right, as in above cheque. Across centre would be printed in large type

THE TREASURY OF THE UNITED STATES OF AMERICA

"The cheque is legal tender for all debts, both public and private," when properly signed in lower right corner with same signature as appears in upper left corner. In lower left corner would be printed the signature of the "Treasurer of the United States." Then the following wording would appear as on common cheques:

Pay to the Order of .... $Dollars.

Of course no amount would be printed on the cheque, for it would be used exactly as today's bank cheques. It would be a domestic cheque, good in any place in the United States or its possessions. A special form would be used for foreign trade.

You would buy the cheque book and pay with your deposits, which would lower your deposits that amount. There would be no charge for the book, for it would be a form of money which the Government would provide the depositors.

If you wanted a $500 chequeing account for the immediate future, the Secretary of your Depository would write that amount on record page which each cheque book would have, and he would sign underneath the amount, and the buyer of the cheque book would sign beneath his signature. There would be lines for entering the date, serial number, person to whom cheque is given, and amount; so that the cheque book owner could keep an accurate record of cheques written; that he might not write a cheque against insufficient or no funds.

The buyer would indicate how many blank cheques he wished to have, and these would be fastened in the book just as travellers cheques are fastened. If he ran out of blank cheques, he would go and buy another book, adjusting the unused balance, if any, of former cheque book; and this would be repeated as often as he ran out of cheques.

Writing a cheque against no funds or insufficient funds, or forging a cheque would be a felony and punishable as counterfeiting. There would be no excuse for writing a cheque against insufficient funds, because the person would be able to keep his balance accurately. Should he write cheques totalling more than his total money written on his cheque book, the last cheque would not be cashed, until he came down and re-adjusted his chequeing funds, it matters not how much he night have to his credit in the Depository. Of course you could go to the depository and draw out cash just as always, and the free use of-the cheque would not be limited, only protected.

There would be no blank cheque pads, as now, lying about in every conceivable place, inviting the witless to write cheques against insufficient funds; or forging a cheque against another person. It would be a felony for any person to be found in possession of a cheque book, which he had not bought from the Depository.

Inasmuch as money would be available in large volume, the people would use cash a great deal more than now. A depositor would exchange deposits for cash and exchange cash for deposits — they would be interchangeable.

They would be dual cheques. They would have the Secretary of the Treasury's signature, making them legal tender money, when you signed it properly; and this would make them your personal cheques. Of course with these cheques flowing freely throughout the nation, you would never buy a postal money order, an express money order, nor a travellers cheque from others. You would use your own cheque instead. That would save the people of the Nation hundreds of millions of dollars a year, and endless hours going to some money order station for a money order. This Treasury cheque in a 3-cent postage envelope would pay a bill anywhere in the Nation.

Congress would compel all persons, firms and corporations to keep their money on deposit with the Depository nearest them, and outlaw anyone lending another cash, and taking a note for it, because there would be no way for Congress to keep informed of loans, their size, and the terms of the loans, etc. This must be known, because the total supply of money must always be under the direct control, and the watchful eyes of Congress.

The Minting and Engraving of Currency

When the Treasurer orders the Bureau of Engraving to mint and print an abundance of currency, rather prodigally, they might mint and print ten times the amount needed, and that would not affect the total volume of money one penny; because the cash would never be on deposit as money; it would never be used, or even considered monetary values, until a depositor drew cash out, and on it re-entering a depositor's hands, it would become actual money, legal tender, and serve in lieu of the personal cheque in making small purchases and paying small bills; and the depositor's account, of course, would have been debited the amount of cash he took out, and when others brought the cash back for deposit, that would raise the deposit level back to normal, and the cash would go back to the vault, to lie there, worthless, as an unsigned cheque, until taken out again by a depositor and put to work.

(Note: I notice that "rags to riches" Texan, Secretary of the Treasury Bob Anderson, is putting "In God We Trust" back on the $1.00 silver certificates. You recall that it was dropped after Civil War, in 1874. After stomping the life out of the South, the Treasury saw no need of calling upon God any more; but now faced with another depression, Bob's putting it back on just $1.00 bills. That's a compliment to us common folks; for only we are supposed to believe in God... a $1.00 bill is about our limit in size. Reminds me of Bob's old grandfather who was shingling his house back in Mississippi. Near the ridge, he began to slip, and cried, "Oh God, save me." His pant's caught on a nail, and the old fellow said, "Never mind, God, a nail stopped me.")

These bills would be similar to a 10 dollar Federal Reserve Note. "Treasury Note" would replace "Federal Reserve Note, and *The Treasury of the United States of America* would appear instead of The United States of America. The picture of a man's head would disappear, and the picture of the Capitol of the United States would be the background. At the bottom of the bill would be *Ten Dollars* only, and the numbers and lettering in the corners would be about the same; but all serial numbers would be left off, with perhaps the seal of the United States superimposed on the picture of the Capitol. There would be no redeemable clause, but beneath the Treasury of the United States would be "This note is legal tender for all debts, both public and private." Both sides of the bill would be identical, and printed reverse, so that when you turned a bill over, the top would be right side up.

These bills would be in $1, $3, $5, $10, $25, $50, and $75, all identical except in figures and *Ten Dollars.* The colours would be different. $1, pink; $3, blue; $5, purple; $10, green; $25, maroon; $50, red, and $75 orange.

The Treasury would have the mints to use a very light, hard, durable metal and mint an abundant supply of small change, nothing higher than a 50-cent coin. These would be different in size, so that these coins would be easily distinguishable. The coin, as with the bill, would have no intrinsic value. Each would be stamped with the "United States of America" at top, and at bottom One Cent, or Ten Cents with large figure in centre, and so on. Both sides of the coin would be stamped the same. "In God We Trust" and other meaningless words would be left off. Instead of a "head" a replica of the capitol building would be stamped on each coin with figure superimposed.

These tokens along with the paper tokens would be in such ample quantities, and they would be so durable, that replacements would be rare; so the mints would not have much to do; and the Government might make a small income by letting them coin souvenirs for the folks.

Expenses of the Government would tumble. You might say that our taxes would jump and jump, but when you cut the Government out of business, and confine its official family to essential routine duties, thousands of unneeded employees would be dropped from the pay rolls, and the soaking of the Government in "foreign" loans, parity payments, and the hundreds of other spillings from Uncle Sammy's pockets, our national expense account would be reduced to an easy load.

You are thinking about what it will cost to "pay out of the general revenues the expenses of the Depositories." Well, remember that you would cease paying the bond holders (bankers) $10 billion a year, and there would be no bonds to pay ultimately. Of course, bankers and bond holders do not expect or want the Government to payoff the bonds. Pay them off and they would not get that $10 billion annually from the tax payers. It would be like taking away from them a great estate that paid them $10,000,000,000 annual rental — these Bonds are one of the geese that now lay the golden eggs, and you would save (taking into the picture the exorbitant rate of interest the Government pays on short-time loans) $20 billion in interest annually. In fact, on public and private debts, the people pay much above $50 billion in interest annually

These Savings Would Remain in the People's Pockets

So this saving alone would many times pay the expenses of the Depositories. But, as I sit here, this morning, any morning, and write this story, constantly there is the thunderous noise our "jet fighter planes" fill the air with. When we get control of our money, arrange amicable international exchange, these army camps all over the world, which we must pay the costs of, will disappear. Great armies will disappear; the Federation of the World will become a reality; and there will be no "ghastly dew from the Nations' airy navies grappling in the central blue; far along the world-wide whisper of the south wind rushing warm, with the standards of the people plunging through the thunder storm (for) the war drums will throb no longer, and the battle- flags (will be) furled in the Parliament of Man, the Federation of the World. Then the common sense of most (the masses) shall hold a fretful realm in awe, and the kindly earth shall slumber, wrapped in universal law."

You are fed daily by radio TV, and Press awful hates, the national and international bankers shovel out to you. Once hate of the Kaiser, then the Hitler, then the Stalin, the Japs were peddled, now the Russians, the Nassars, the Tartars, the Chinese are held up in scorn that we may hate them. And back of it all is "international money," the desire of each nation to control. Until the Russian revolution in 1917, all of our national life, Russia had been our bosom friend; and never a note of her feudalism; but when the masses revolted, and their leaders set up "communism," and quit using our money, the bankers and international money lenders began a systematic hate campaign, trying to keep the people hating the Russians; because after all is said and done, the only power on earth that the despoilers of men fear is the aroused enlightened masses. They have no fear of brainwashed people.

These people who are leading our war manoeuvres — now a perpetual war — a cold war when not hot with shooting — not only keep the masses in bondage, but make billions, aye, trillions out of wars. Today, with no Nation on earth wanting to make battle with us, we keep calling Nassar, King Saud, the Russians sons of bitches, and continue to drop those ghastly bales from the central blue, as a threat and warning that "you'll get it, if you attack us."

This insane thing is costing the people of the United States $65 billion a year, or $130 billion every two years as against $7 billion on all other government expenditures! With the Federation of the World, there would be no "national armies," just a small police force under the Federation of the World.

The *Reader's Digest* carried a story the other day about the miraculous comeback of the West Germans. It said that West Germany had made a miraculous comeback, and gave three reasons:

(a)   money pouring in from the United States,
(b)   no army to support, and
(c)   hard-working Germans.

Then it said that the Minister of Finance had squeezed the water out of the Reichsmark, etc. Suppose we could squeeze that $65 billion a year out of our budget! We could as we would squeeze (if the Congress takes over the creation and control of money) the $10 billion out of Bond taxes.

Let Congress take over the creation of money, the cashing and clearing of our cheques, with the safeguards we have set forth above, and there will always be sound money, fluid money, ample money, universal confidence in our money, and all thought of "bank failures" will forever disappear.

It is astounding that millions of people in all depressions and bank failures lose billions of deposits, yet grumble to themselves, and go right on doing business with the same gang who has robbed them for

150 years here in the United States... it was more decent of the Government from the closing of the Second United States Bank by Andrew Jackson to the passage of the Reserve Act in 1913, under Woodrow Wilson, because they merely sat idly by and let private bankers go ahead in their boom and bust muddling of the people's economy than since 1913, because in the Reserve Act Congress adopted as law the rules bankers wrote, and permitted the impression to grow in the minds of the people that the Government creates and issues all of our money.

Finally let me point out to you that governments have uniformly punished severely counterfeiters because adding new and uncontrolled money to a nation's money supply brings the counterfeiter into competition with the producers of goods, and every dollar added above the existing supply cheapens every man's dollar. It lets the man who does not produce or serve, take of the products of others and their services without giving value received in return. They fight counterfeiters because it is an axiom in money that every time you increase the volume of money in circulation, you lower the buying power of the dollar.

That is the basic reason why we should forever destroy the debt dollar. It is a phoney dollar, and not only competes with the sound, honest dollar, but utterly destroys the fixed value of a dollar.

So accustomed to the creation of money by making loans and buying investment obligations have we become, that even Congressmen are praising our "debt dollar." Debt has always been the enemy of sound business practices, the bane of stable governments. The wisest plan ever set up for industry, business) individuals, and governments is the "pay-as-you-go" plan.

Corporation fighting to lower their income 'tax burdens uniformly have pleaded "we must have funds for replacement, improvements, advancements," which simply says, "we must pay-as-we-go to be successful."

Therefore, there should be no "debt-created dollar." When the Treasury (when there comes a need for greater volume of money to meet the business demands), gives the Government credit for say $10,000,000, this would not be a debt dollar; for there would be no bonds issued as evidence of a debt, as now under the Reserve System. It would be all of the people adding more dollars to the money supply, that there might be enough to meet their business demands. The dollar would immediately begin serving all of the people, because the Government would cheque it out to all of the people who sold goods to the Government, or served the Government, thereby saving for the time being the collection of $10,000,000 in taxes. These dollars would find a welcome place in industry, not as cheaters of the old dollars, but as helpers making it easier for the old dollars to carry the economic load of the Nation.

As often as, business increased to such volume that the current volume of deposits would be inadequate to carry on the Nation's business; or, should an emergency come as in the 30s, or due to war, and there became a need for greater funds than taxes and revenues provided for the Government, Congress would by Act instruct the Treasurer to give the Government deposit credit for the money needed, say $100,000,000,000 (billion). This would be chequed out to the citizens of the Nation for goods and services, and would immediately become earned dollars, and remain in the hands of the people, enabling the Government to meet the emergency; and when the emergency was over, Congress would ascertain the period over which the Nation could retire these excess deposits, and, say it is 20 years, each year the Treasury would fail to take deposit credit for $5 billion, which would restore the volume of deposits to peace-time level. AND THERE WOULD BE NO $100 BILLION IN U.S. BONDS ISSUED TO PRIVATE CORPORATIONS. It would be then as now, except the bonds would not be printed! That would be a saving of the principal $100 billion, and $3 billion a year interest. No, no my fellow-citizens; not a debt dollar, but an earned dollar, and these $10,000,000 would enter the hands of those who earned them, because each had rendered service or sold the Government goods. And every person thereafter who would receive one of them would have earned it.

The dollars themselves would be as negligible as the white slips of paper put into voters hands when they are called upon to vote in an election. The act of putting them into the voters' hands would mean nothing. The writing of the name of person on it and placing it in the hat would give it value. When the Government was given credit for the $10,000,000, it was like putting the slips of white paper on the voting table; but when the Government wrote cheques and sent them to those who sold goods or rendered the Government service, those $10 million became actual money in circulation... the best money in the world, "earned dollars."

CHAPTER XVI

SETTING UP LENDING AGENCIES

Now that we have killed the bankers' goose that for a thousand years has been laying them golden eggs; increasing in number of eggs as the years passed — just as the domestic hens of the long ago like the birds of the fields, laid only one batch of eggs a year, in the springtime when all life was multiplying; but now continue throughout the year, laying sometimes over 300 eggs a year; so has this bankers' goose that laid golden eggs: from a few eggs a year in the middle ages, she has come to lay billions a year — we must provide for the poor fellows.

They have always told us simps that they are lending us the depositors' money, and we have believed them! They never had the nerve to say we are lending *our* money. A small banker, whose capital was $10,000, said to me: "We have to lend the depositors' money. Our capital is only $10,000; we have loaned $65,000; and our depositors' deposits are $68,000!"

The Government will let them lend only their own deposits, and such deposits as other depositors may subrogate to them for lending. These must be kept on the books of the Depositories, and be disbursed by cheque.

Since we have executed the death sentence on the word banking, of course, they can't open up banks; so the Congress will give their business a name, and outline the rules of their lending deposit credits (they will not be permitted to lend money-currency, coin or bills.)

I suggest that the Congress give them the name of Deposit Lenders, prefixed with any descriptive term they may choose, say "The Austin Deposit Lenders; but always keep it clear before the public that they are lending deposits — their deposits and such deposits as other depositors' may subrogate to them (for interest) to lend. Let the word money go too.

Let's emphasize that the lending of money, deposits, is a private right; and that we are going to guarantee that private corporations or lending agencies shall be protected in the exercise of this private right.

It shall be provided that when the Lenders make a loan, they shall use a special form of note, provided by the Depositories, which shall recite the terms of the loan, the principal and rate of interest, the time period of the note if it is to be paid in one lump sum; or the instalment periods and the amounts of the instalments, if paid off in instalments. The borrower signs the note, and such mortgages or security requirements as the lender may exact, and hands them to the lender; the lender then writes a cheque on a special cheque form provided by the Depository, and hands it to the borrower. On this cheque are all the details of the loan, listing the chattels put up for security of the note, etc.

The borrower takes the cheque to the Depository the lenders must not be an adjunct of the Depository or in the same building The Depository gives the borrower credit for the cheque, and debits the lender's account an equal amount. The Depository makes a photostat of the cheque, marks it paid, and puts it with other cheques the lender has given to other borrowers; and at the end of the month, these "paid" cheques will be mailed to the lender, for his files.

The photostat goes into the Depository files, and the face of the loan, the instalments, and all pertinent items on the cheque, are consolidated with all other lenders' loans handled through that Depository, and sent periodically to The Treasury of the United States. All depositories will make similar reports, and from these reports consolidated, Congress may know at all times, the total loans of deposits the lenders have made, total unpaid instalments, etc.

This information is vital to the economy of the Nation, and keeps Congress alerted to malpractices which might turn up. This would put the "loan shark" out of business, because it would be made a felony for any person or firm to lend another person *cash,* and take his note for it. Only deposits could be loaned. Congress, of course, would fix interest rates.

Then as a follow-up, and a completing of every loan, when the borrower made a payment, even a partial payment, on his note, he would have to use a special cheque provided by the Depository, which would have listed amount borrowed, amount still due, and the balance due after this cheque is credited to the lender; and when the lender presented the cheque for deposit with the Depository, the Depository would also photostat it, and handle it exactly as it did the lender's cheque, only it would go back to the borrower for his "receipt" and files. That would make money lending simple, direct, safe for both lender and borrower.

Money lending, or we ought to always say "Deposit Lending," for "money" is and has been so long associated in our minds with currency, coin and bills, that when we say money lending, we naturally see money changing hands. We have found that cash (coin and bills) is not money, a thing of value; but is a token to be used instead of a cheque against deposits, as a convenience, because it does not require signature or endorsement, and will be accepted by all sellers.

To repeat, Deposit Lending is a very essential part of our economy; for there will always be those who prodigally spend their income, spend more than they make, or even just as much as they make. There will always be thrifty people who spend less than they make, and these naturally accumulate deposit credits they do not wish to spend. Sickness, or some other emergency may confront the prodigal spender, and he must have deposits that he may eat, or pay hospital bills, so it is a service to him and to humanity in general for the lender, the thrifty fellow, to lend him some deposits to tide him over the emergency.

So deposit lending being a public necessity, those who have saved should be protected in their loans, and be paid for the use of their deposit credits, because these deposit credits are work translated into deposits.

Under Careful Supervision Congress May Increase Deposits Naturally lenders are going to run out of deposits because each time they make a loan, they will reduce their deposit balance the face of the loan. Too they have been used to an unlimited lending range, limited only by the whims of the Reserve Authorities. This could rarely occur.

But now, under The Treasury Depository System, the Congress would know the entire story of their lending, its extent and its coverage; so if Congress felt that additional deposits to the credit of the lender, or lenders would be in the interest of the public's good, and not unduly increase the volume of money, Congress would say to the lenders, "Give the Treasury your note for the $10 million, and attached collateral worth three times the loan, say $30 million; and the Treasurer will give you a cheque which you may deposit in your home Depository, which will increase your loan range $10 million — not $50 million, as is the case under the Reserve System. And all of that $10 million would be earmarked for lending. An officer of the Deposit Lenders could not cheque out $5,000, and take the family on a world tour, or buy a yacht, or a ranch. It would be for lending; and the regulation of lending would enable the Government to know that every dollar went to borrowers on loans. The lenders would be compelled to live on the interest paid to them by borrowers.

At the end of the loan period, say ten years, the lenders would have to give the Government a cheque against their deposits for $10 million, which would lower their lending deposit back to pre-loan period. The Treasury would not give the Government credit for the $10 million, which would automatically restore the total deposit credits to the pre-loan period, unless the Nation needed the additional deposits. As the lenders paid the Government $300,000 interest each year, totalling $3 million, the Treasurer would place this to the credit of the Government, which would be spent by the Government in paying for services and goods. It would be an "income" to the Government, to all of us, and would help defray the expenses of the Government. It would not be new deposits.

Now, that would be putting the shoe on the other foot. Under the Reserve System, Uncle Sam must borrow his own credit, and not only pay interest on it, but pay the principal, or continue paying interest forever. Unlike the Bankers the Government would not take title to the $10 million loan, but would cancel it out, that it might not remain in circulation to cheapen other deposit credits. And the lender's note would not be for sale — it would lie in Treasury until paid.

That would forever take the Government out of the borrowing category; it would forever stop the people's having to pay taxes to pay interest on a "national debt." There would never be a national debt.

The Deposit Lenders would be protected in their field of lending, because the Government could not lend

Deposits to any person, corporation, or Nation, except to the lenders, as shown above. And this would be a creative act.

Then Congress, the Government, would create "money" or deposits, and not lend it; and the lenders would lend deposits, but could not create them. It would keep the Government out of "business" and would prevent the lenders' pyramiding the Government's "capital."

It would kill this "Creditalistic System" we have lived under, suffered under for 150 years. We would have no system; we would have the mechanics of money simplified to the lowest point. As shown, there would be no central clearing house; there would be direct connection between any Depository and any other Depository in the Nation; and The Treasury would be the Central Agency which would handle the Government's cheques, keep its deposits, print and mint money, the Depository cheques of the various forms, and keep all Depositories supplied with ample amounts and quantities of each. It would have a supervisory control over the Depositories, but everything it did would be in obedience to the will of the Congress of the United States.

Wouldn't that be the finest thing you could imagine: Our nation not a debtor nation? No private corporation with the power of life or death over all of us. No 19 men, private citizens, bankers who have but one purpose, to make money for their stockholders, meeting tri-weekly, an arbitrarily putting more money in circulation, or siphoning it out.

Wouldn't it be good to send Morgan & Company back to New York, not as the masters of the Nation, but as run-of-the-mill Deposit Lenders? Make Washington and Congress at our Capital masters of our deposits, and not New York, and the 19 private bankers? And send the Morgan & Company's stock market angel,

Barnie Baruch, back to his Hobcaw, his 17,000-acre Shangri La where he has entertained every president since Taft, and leading members of the House and Senate, as he coyly and masterfully brainwashed these public officials; where he entertained President Wilson and members of Congress when he masterfully manoeuvred the First Reserve Act through Congress, in 1913; where he entertained Roosevelt in 1934-35 when he manoeuvred a rewriting of the Reserve Act, exalting his beloved corporation stock above gold, giving us a Corporation-Stock-Standard for our money; where he has just finished entertaining Eisenhower and the members of Congress, securing the rewriting of the Reserve Act, omitting much, and adding much more, under the deceptive title "An Act-to Amend and Revise the Statutes Governing Financial Institutions and Credit," studiously refusing to use the term Reserve Bank, because bankers know that the sins of "banking" have about caught up with them?

Isn't it good to find that the strength and power and stability of our Government, and not chattels give our money (Deposits) soundness; and not fictitious portfolios prepared by bankers to deceive the Government and the public?

Isn't it good to discover that not the bankers' boasted wealth, or resources, has given us a stable government, a reasonably sound money? Congressman Patman, in 1943, still fighting to protect the people from: the greed of the bankers, said:

Not Private Corporations'
But The Government's Guarantee

"The present banking system, through the use of the Government's credit ... proposes to finance the war (that is the Reserve bankers do) and issue more than $240 billion in money, and every bit of it will be issued on the banks - all banks combined — $8 billion capital and surplus *and the Government's credit.* Of course it will be the Government's credit that will make it secure, as the $8 billion will be insufficient security ... so the Government must pay interest for the use of its own credit."

Think of bankers saying that *our* $8 billion capital and surplus are ample security for issuing $240 billion deposit credits; when they always demand three times the loan in chattels as security when they make you a loan. Here they are saying our $8 billion is ample security for the $240 billion, just one-thirtieth the value of the new deposits it proposed to create! Of course their wealth would be — but it is not obligated.

Won't it be fine, fellow slaves to the banking system, to have the chains struck from our necks and legs, and be free men again, with no overlord except our Congress which we choose every two years?

Think of not paying annually that $10 billion interest on a debt we gave the bankers; and then finally extinguishing the debt, and as a people, as a nation, be free of national debt thence forward.

Having the $10 billion deposits provided by the Congress for the lenders to lend the people, earmarked "good for loans only," fits in with the Act of Congress setting up lending agencies, corporations for a specific purpose, the lending of deposits to borrowers, which would provide that no lending agency could buy corporation stock or other investment obligations. They could only lend deposits to borrowers. If a person wanted to gamble in the stock market, he would have to do it on his own. This would take money lenders, who are chartered for public service, the lending of money, out of the speculative field, out of stock market gambling.

And they could not buy corporation stock, or real estate, or any other thing with their deposits. But you would, on first impulse say, "But that would be interfering with a man's private right to do as he pleases with his money-lend it, or spend it for whatever he wanted." No this would not interfere with a person's, a man's private rights. It would only control "that person," a corporation; and since the Nation creates a corporation, it has the right to say what the corporation mayor may not do. If a lender decides he had rather gamble his money in the Stock Market, he will have to withdraw from the corporation, and go it as a person, just a man

This would limit the money available to play around gambling on the stock market to such a trickle, it would kill the business of selling watered stock, which is the stock-in-trade with stock exchanges, and bankers.

After World War I, when we were "booming" again, the Borah Committee (of the United States Senate) exhaustively investigated this watered-stock racket, and they found that corporations had watered their stock from a few percent of their legitimate stock, to as much as 168 times their legitimate stock.

In 1932-33 Doheney, chief of the Cities Service Gas Stations, issued $30 million in stock, with the usual fraudulent statement: "to extend and improve our service." When the $30 million cheque came in for the stock, Doheney promptly credited his own personal account with $16 million. He bought, with $11 million, the *Kansas City Star.* It is a common practice now.

When a corporation sells a new issue of stock, the officials may cheque that stock out to buy anything from a purple cow to a million dollar addition of equipment.

That's phoney, hot-cheque money competing with the people's earned dollars.

There could be no lending agencies failures; for every loan they made would be secured by ample chattels; and the Congress would trim the interest rate to that point where the lenders could not take usury from the borrowers. There could be no watered stock sold. Hence there would be no profit in stock exchanges, and they would disappear.

Morgan & Company, as with many smaller banks, is a stock-market promoter and gambler first, and banker second. They do not use their banking facilities to stimulate honest, essential industry, but to promote profits through the stock market. Bankers use the stock markets to swell their incomes just as they lend money.

CHAPTER XVII

THIS MUST BE DONE FIRST

In Texas, and I suspect it is true in all states, we live under an oligarchy. Only three men dominate and dictate what the Texas Legislature mayor may not do. The people nowhere in our political system damning Texas have any voice, beyond the local precinct, and even there some henchman of the oligarchy "presides" at all meetings.

Have you ever stopped to ponder the fact that you never know how many ballots are actually cast at any election? How many are counted and how many are thrown out; how many were "cast" by dead, or nonexistent voters? You certainly know that every person with sound mind, over the age of 21, has a legal right to vote. Aye, more, have you ever stopped to ponder that above your "legal right to vote," in a democracy *You Must Vote*. That to refuse to inform yourself on candidates and issues and then fail to vote, you are as guilty of treason, as much as a slacker who refuses to take up arms in defence of his country, and lends aid and comfort to the enemy?

Certainly you know that as long as the rich are permitted to put up millions to elect "their" man, and then follow him to Austin (or your state capitol, or our National capitol) and there spend millions brainwashing your lawmakers, spent through lobbyists, buying copy in newspapers, and journals, time on the radio and TV, you the masses, are not going to be represented either in legislation or administration of the Government.

Then we must turn to our only weapon, our ballots. It must be an informed ballot. It must be cast with the full assurance that it will be counted as a ballot, and not thrown out on the slightest mark "mutilation" the election holders may discover. You may be a Ph.D., and yet cast as ignorant ballot as the most illiterate person, and many of you do; because you "are above taking an active part in politics - it is so dirty," and keep your noses stuck in some musty tome, and never ascertain what manner of man is, asking your ballot.

Let us rectify our own shortcomings cast a ballot at every election, and not let the oligarchy man our election staff. If we do they will defeat the wisest and most thoughtful ballot. So that the ballot box should ever be in the hands of our citizens, no man or woman should be permitted to help hold elections covering more than two years, within a period of twelve years, and that where there are two parties to be voted upon, the holders of the elections should be equally divided between or among the parties, and when issues are to be voted upon, the pros and cons should be equally numbered on the list.

This would give every man and woman a chance to *give* his country that highest service, helping to keep the ballot box clean. I have been casting ballots every election for 57 years, and as the years have passed the faces holding the election have come to remain the same for years and years. They grow "old in the service," yet they hobble to the polls, and sit with wizened faces for us to gaze it. Here is the danger: If the election holders are the same year in and year out, they come to a common understanding, and the "leaders" can put over the gravest abuses of the ballot box.

That every person may vote, all places of business should by law be closed at 9:00 a.m., and remain closed until 3:00 p.m. that every voter might have time and leisure to go vote. The ballot boxes should open at 9 :00 a.m., and close at 3 :00 p.m. and the ballots should be counted, returns filled in and the "locked boxes" should be in the county clerk's office before 6:00 p.m., same day. That this might be done, no election precinct should have over 100 voters, and these precincts should be compact, no gerrymandering allowed; and the manager of the election, being one of the 100 voters, could easily know each by name, and there would be no possible chance of "smart" citizens voting at two or more boxes each election; and there would be no long line standing in line waiting to vote when the doors closed.

For a voter to say, "I have not read the amendment," or the issue to be voted upon, should be a misdemeanour, punishable by fine. It is the *duty* of every voter to inform himself, and *vote*, and when he fails he is striking a death blow at democracy. It is *not* your *right* to *vote*; it is *your duty to vote*, and when you fail either to inform yourself that you may cast an informed ballot, or fail to vote, you are guilty of a crime against your country.

The informing yourself on issues is easy, for all matters submitted to the voters, for adoption or rejection, by law, must be published in full in newspaper with circulation in your precinct. But, that is not true with candidates. Before a proposition is submitted to the voters, the Legislature, or Commissioners' Court, or City Aldermen have argued and thrashed the issue out; but when I get ready to run for Governor, or any office down to constable, nobody but me and the few or many who want me to be elected (because they hope to use me) know my qualifications, or lack of qualifications, to hold the office to which I aspire. We have had ignoramuses, who have taken so little interest in government before they announce, that they seldom voted, to announce for Governor, pay the $100 filing fee, and go out to "win votes."

There should be some method devised that would enable the State to ascertain the qualifications of a person to hold the office he seeks. And this should cover age, background, character, reputation, residence, even personality. and this information along with the candidate's own story about himself, and the story of what his neighbours might want to offer for or against him — all whipped into a story covering the man's qualifications, character, etc. ... and these stories of all candidates offering at the election for office, should *be* published in book at State expense, when within a state, or at National expense when it should be a person seeking National office, and a copy put in the hands of every voter, or family of voters, in the areas included within the territory covered.

I have often suggested this, and supposed-to-be thoughtful and informed men have demurred: "But how are you going to find a body of men who would be fair and honest about it?" And I reply: "Well, let's just quit, and let the evil forces run the government. But, even barbers have a test; the person wanting to cut your hair and shave your face must pass before he can become a barber "in good standing." If this can't be done, let's abandon all qualifications required of a person before being employed as a teacher, and let the best looking, the glibbest talking person, even though we know he is a rogue, get employment as teacher, if the school board wants to hire him."

How voters and Not Money May Control

Then make it a felony for a candidate to accept "campaign expenses," free radio and newspaper and TV publicity; or for any person to offer the money, or to pay for the TV, radio and newspaper advertising. He could not buy his own time, on radio or TV, nor buy "articles" in newspapers. He would be permitted to spend as much as he pleased of his own cash in going from place to place and speaking to groups and shaking the voters' hands. Person to person contact is good.

This would put an end to the candidate saying, "If I can get financial backing I shall run for the United States Senate," because he would not get it; unless he and the contributor ran a risk of facing jail and fine. With his story in concise language, the story of his neighbours and the commission's review of his qualifications, integrity, and fitness to hold the office, in the hands of every voter in the State, or County, or district, or precinct, there would be no need for him to "win votes."

And there is one avenue to winning votes that *must* be blocked, and that is the "grapevine" wireless. No candidate could make charges against his opponent. He would have to run on his own merits. And if he or any other person should circulate a lie, good or bad, about another candidate, and the instigator or repeater of the lie could be discovered, no time limit on the case, he would be guilty of a felony, and sent to jail.

Adopt these simple, easily applied rules covering our elections, and money will cease to rule; and crooks and incompetents can never hold office. One person would be automatically barred, the person convicted of a felony or malfeasance in office.

This approach to the election of officers would necessitate staggering their tenures of office. As it now is, we have every four years all Congressmen, perhaps one of the Senators, and all state offices from constable to Governor and State Supreme Court justice running, and the result is that the public becomes hypnotized by the best looking, most endowed-with-cash candidate, and forgets the rest. Since 1932, especially, we give full attention to the National candidate, and let our lower offices be filled by slip-ins by default.

So we should every two years choose, on a state and national level, the Congressmen up that year, the Legislators, and the City Aldermen, and each should be chosen for six years, with one- third re-elected every two years, which would give us a rotating body of legislators, with never over one-third fresh from the people. And at end of tenure of office, no official would be eligible for re-election to the office he is quitting, or any other office within two years. Only legislation should occupy our minds during this election year.

The Governors and President with all elective judges would be chosen for 8-year terms of office, and one-half of the Governors would be chosen each four years. The President would be chosen between the elections for governors, so that they would not conflict for publicity and interest with each other.

All county and local officers should be chosen on odd years, so as to never be submerged beneath state and national candidates. All elections on amendments and propositions should be held on odd years so that no other public interest could interfere.

Our greatest menace in a democracy is corporations. The father of democracy in the United States, Thomas Jefferson, fought with all of his might to have another amendment adopted at the time the first ten were adopted. He gave as his reason for wanting the people to adopt his amendment: "If the state licenses men to do a certain thing, they will be so much more powerful as a corporation than the individual that they can oppress him, destroy his business." Therefore he wanted to forever outlaw the granting to any group a special permit or license.

When we look at our steel industry, our automotive industry, our oil industry, our electrical industry, our banking system, our transportation system, and now our marketing system, controlled 100 percent by corporations, we need no further argument to convince us that corporations should go. Jefferson went further in his fight to outlaw corporations, he said that corporations would grow so powerful that they could and would challenge the Government itself. And that has come true. The Federal *Reserve* System, and not the Government rules America and is now compelling the Government to spend $32 billion annually in equipping a military force that can rule and dominate the world. Not only can corporations buy the most astute lawyers (and most of our Congressmen are corporation lawyers), but they hire our best scientific brains.

The young daring Frenchman, Tocqueville, in 1831, just forty years after Jefferson failed to outlaw corporations, after a visit of several weeks in America wrote:

"In an orderly and peaceable democracy (and we were a peaceable democracy then) like the United States, where men can not enrich themselves by war, by public office, or by political confiscation (that was before the Federal Reserve System of 1913) love of wealth mainly drives them into business and manufacturing." How far from being true today. Take profit out of war and war would cease.

The corporation man will say that you could not run the country without *us*. No man would put his money in a general partnership. And that is what Thomas Jefferson said: "If any enterprise is too big for a general partnership to handle, it should be done by the Government" ... and the Government followed that advice at once - it began to build post roads, and to establish post offices, and to provide the nation its money. But corporations came in and took over the providing of its money, creating the debt-dollar money. Today in the richest country in the world in natural resources, with the most aggressive, virile people on earth, business can not run one year on its own capital, it must return again and again to the banks for money to keep their businesses going.

Cut out this fallacy of "mass production," and let all industry drop back into the "small operators' hands" and prosperity would become universal and satisfying. No "great" industry completely fabricates its machinery today. Even Ford, General Motors, Western Electric, all of them subcontract parts, and then assemble them.

Corporation newspapers and journals should go. No newspaper should circulate beyond its community, (not even state coverage - then a few in New York, would not brainwash the rest of us with their political rand social nostrums. The Morgan Company could not rule America.

Our fathers, 100 years ago were fighting Wall Street, and if banking is continued, Wall Street will be our masters in 2057. The small business man will disappear. Three classes would encompass all of the people, (a) the big, industries, and (b) the hirelings, and (c) the rest who would be on the dole.

A Final Assurance

In all that I have written, I have had but one thought in mind, and that has been to let you see the operations of the Federal Reserve Banking System, and to point out to you the tremendous cost this private corporation is piling up against the producing people of the United States.

That it is unconstitutional for the United States to turn over to a private corporation the "coining of money, and the regulating the value thereof," is evident without argument to anyone who will take time to read the "powers" granted to Congress in the Constitution.

I have not sought to bring in religion or world cabals as productive of this money situation in the United States. I blame no foreign nation for the situation. I do not wish to detract your mind from the main issue, and that is that the Federal Reserve System is robbing the people yearly of hundreds of billions of dollars, and that the few men directing its operations are mad men, drunk on power, and obsessed with an ambition for power... money, gold per se has no appeal to them, it is the feeling of power that inspires them to greater and still greater crimes. Money never inspired a king; it was the feeling of power which he held over a people that urged him on. And this is the urge behind the Federal Reserve System.

It must be thrilling to those who would rule to see the drying up or flooding of the Nation's money supply, and watch and hear the people's shouts of joy, or pleadings for bread. Certainly I am sure that when they see men of all calibres bending their knees in recognition of their power, when they see the Congress meekly do their biddings, when they rebuke a president and he takes rebuke humbly, that most dominant characteristic of mankind, the desire to be top dog, must have full flowering. From the small grocery to the vast industrial empires, there is someone in the organization who repeats, that his underlings may not forget, "I'm boss around here."

The course of the Federal Reserve System could not be dominated by greed, for greed can be satiated and certainly the ownership of the United States does that; it must be impelled and dominated by the desire to go one's own way without obstruction or interference. And this desire has never been satiated.

If the feeling of power and a desire to crack the whip over their fellowmen had not been the ruling passion of their minds, if they had been prompted by a great ambition to obey that deeper, finer impulse of man, to help all mankind, the Federal Reserve System could have been, even in private hands, the most beneficent institution men could desire; for certainly the men directing the Federal Reserve System could have turned great producers like Ford, Wilson, et al, to the task of seeing that every citizen of the United States should be educated, well-clothed, well-housed, and well-entertained; and they would have gotten as big kick out of seeing this product passing over their assembly lines as they have watching cars, TV s, gadgets pouring forth in an endless stream.

I believe that the Congress could do that. At least, the oath they take commands them to do this. If every citizen in the United States would make it a rule to read the Constitution at the breakfast table, when all members of the family are assembled; then repeat the "Preamble" each day, especially just before taking any important step, within one generation the might and power and brawn and know-how of America would convert us into a beehive of happy, industrious, prosperous (individually) people, and that our war engines would be beaten into implements of industry, while no nation on earth would be seeking to destroy us.

Being such good friends to ourselves, we would in turn be such good friends to the rest of the world, that no one would hate and seek to destroy, but all nations would seek to emulate our way of life. Read in current *Reader's Digest* the threatening situation growing up between Canada and the United States ... and the core of it is that our oil men have gone in and practically taken over Canada's oil and gas resources ... not as men bent on pouring wealth into Canada but with a definite purpose of siphoning her wealth out of Canada.

Were these men dominated with a desire to see Canada enjoy her natural resources, they would go with their know how, and not with their "power of dollars," and that almost ideal relationship which has existed since we gained our independence, would be reaching new glories.

I am not concerned about what other nations think about us, so much as I am about what we think of ourselves. I believe that when we set up an ideal democracy here, the rest of the world will seek to emulate us.

The Congress of the United States can create money and keep the people's deposits and cash and clear their cheques, as a "public service," directed toward meeting the conditions of our "general welfare," without special favours to anyone, with all citizens enjoying an equal service, as they administer the post office business. They would no more think of denying the smallest citizen enjoyment of the privilege of borrowing money than they would think of denying the smallest citizen the privilege of sending a letter through the mails.

That's why the Constitution provides that; Congress shall have the power to coin money and regulate the value thereof.

The battle is not against past leaders and present leaders, nor do we have to concern ourselves about foreign powers... our task is a simple, practical one ... let Congress take back the power to coin money and regulate the value thereof, which they have so carelessly entrusted to men who are impelled by an acquisitive mind, with all love of mankind shoved far back into the limbo of forgotten things. Congress can set this house of money in order. Congress must set this house in order. Nothing else will meet the issues of life; nothing else in life can grow to full fruition until this is done.

This is not a political issue. There is no ground for thinking as a liberal or a conservative, as a democrat or a republican. This is not a battle between the rich and the poor. It is meeting that standard of the "general welfare" we all subscribe to and proclaim as the goal of America.

CHAPTER XVIII

INFLATION AND FEATHERBEDDING

Permit me in this closing chapter to emphasize two facts: (a) cash, bills and coins, is not a part of our volume of money; (b) Private banking corporations and not the Government and labour are responsible for high prices. — high wages, high rents, high taxes, cheap money — inflation. On page 27, Reserve book (1939) we read: "There are two principal ways by which any individual gets paper money and coin. Either he draws it out of the bank and has it charged to his account; or he is paid for his labour, his services, or his merchandise with money that has been drawn out of a bank by someone else."

On page 19, same book, we find: "Currency is actually used for only a small part of the country's total volume of payments, the greater part being effected by the use of bank (personal) cheques."

Since one must cheque over to the bank a portion of his deposits that he may get cash, then it stands to reason that personal cheques and cash are interchangeable, and not supplementary. The last edition of this book, 1954, which seeks to camouflage the whole picture, says on page 5: "When a person has $10 in his pocket and $100 in his chequeing account in the bank he is in a position to spend $110." Then on page 7: "For a general idea of money, the two kinds — pocket money and demand money — should be considered together."

The author forgot that he or someone else had chequed the $10 out of the bank.

Both of those statements are designed to camouflage the fact that there is but one kind of money today, bank deposits. If we are to consider different "kinds" of money, we must list more than two kinds, we must list all express and postal money orders, all travellers cheques, cashiers' cheques, because all of these forms of "money" are good in any market of the United States, when bought and signed.

And to limit our volume of money just to the "demand deposits," is the sorriest sort of reckoning. Time deposits may easily be transferred over to the demand column. And the same is true of savings deposits, and many other "deposits" hidden in different nooks, and cached in many secret places. Any form of monetary obligation may be quickly and easily converted into demand deposits, therefore nobody, and I mean *nobody* knows the volume of all of the monetary funds listed under the many headings. Yet, to arrive at the volume of money we must ascertain all of these funds, and reach a grand total. To do so would alarm even the informed in the creative field of money.

Cash does not enter that picture, because it is exchangeable with cheques, bank deposits. You transform anyone of the several kinds of deposits into another, by changing the figures from one column to another; but when you draw money out of the bank, you have your account debited an equivalent amount, and while you have the cash in your hand, you use it rather than a personal cheque.

It is the sorriest sort of cover up to say that we have just two kinds of money, cash and demand deposits, when a child should know that the only difference between time deposits and demand deposits is a mere matter of time, and that at any time you may have the banker transfer your time deposits to your demand deposits, and you may proceed to cheque against it immediately. So fellow-citizens, when you take just the volume of cash plus the volume of demand deposits for our total volume of money, you have only a small percentage of our money supply. The time deposits, the savings deposits, the billions of bank credit which may be quickly converted into deposits; aye, you may convert your investment obligations, from a promissory note to U.S. Bonds" quickly into *new* deposits, swelling the, volume of money, and all of it sends the total volume of money skyward.

If you accept such spurious reasoning as that we have just "two kinds of money, cash and demand deposits," then why not go a step further and admit that there are many millions in the demand deposit columns that are never chequed out, and as far as the circulating money is concerned, it too is "time" dead deposits.

All writers who are assiduously seeking to have the similes of bankers, and enjoy their crumbs, seek by might and main to keep the true volume of money a secret to the people. Let this be said as a final fact: Our volume of money is the total value of all monetary investment obligations which may be easily and quickly converted into bank deposits" subject to cheque, plus the hundreds of billions of deposits on the books of banks and all financial institutions.

And remember this: there is no more reason for adding the cash in a bank's vaults to the volume of deposits to arrive at its total money supply, than there is to add the possible total of personal cheques which might be written. If you would understand banking, money as it now is and functions, forget about cash, and keep your eye on bank deposits.

The Hoary Lie of Inflation

Now let's examine inflation. As an introductory lesson, let's quote a "Professor of Business Administration and Retailing at the American University, Washington, D.C., a Mr. Harold B. Weiss, a former vice-president of Macy's, New York.

"Unless, the major economic trend of the last 25 years in this country is reversed, the only free enterprise system left in the world will bleed itself to death. *It is not a depression that threatens us; the imminent danger is inflation...* We are now caught in a vicious circle. The more the Government spends, the more inflation; the more inflation, the higher are *government* expenses. Another *vicious* circle is the continuing increase in labour costs, which bring higher prices, more inflation, then still, higher wages, until the bubble bursts, as it must." He knows that *Government* spending does not increase money supply. Only *government* borrowing!

The professor is either ignorant of money, economics, and causes and effects, or he is criminally trying to brainwash the people. There is not a grain of truth in a single assertion quoted above. The "professor" leads out the old, jaded nags, *Government* spending, and Labor greed.

Let's look at *Government* spending. Who is to blame for it? Why must we keep a $32 billion military program going? To protect the labouring masses? The common people? Nay, verily. It is to protect the crowd the professor is seeking to *serve,* international *investors.* Are you willing, Mr. Weiss, to disband our military forces? Are you ready to dry up the trickle that goes to all other agencies of the government, a bagatelle, three and a half billion?

If we are going to jump on Uncle Sam for spending, what about the corporation spending, the Reserve Banks buying investment obligations, the hundreds of billions in loans made to persons, firms, corporations, municipalities, states, which is new money, inflation? What of the Reserve Open Market Committee, who may buy, any day, corporation stock running into many millions of dollars, and giving the corporation a cheque against no funds, which on being deposited in a commercial bank swells the volume of money, face of the cheque, and bank credits five times the cheque?

On page 39, 1939 Reserve book, we find that "The aggregate deposits in the banking system as a whole (not just demand deposits but the aggregate, all deposits in all accounts) represent mainly funds lent by banks or paid by banks for securities, mortgages, and other forms of investment obligations... the proceeds go on deposit to be disbursed by cheque, and aggregate deposits are increased."

During the last 25 years, Mr. Weiss, there must have been many trillions of dollars in loans, made, U.S. Bonds, notes, and other investment obligations bought by banks, and every time they made a loan or bought an investment obligation, they gave the seller deposit credits, which were *new* deposits, added to the volume at the time the loan was made.

That's the nigger in the wood pile, dear readers. High prices, high wages, high taxes are not inflation. They are the result of money inflation. We have hundreds of billions too much money in circulation, on deposit, cached in many secret niches.

Of course every time the Government issues bonds, the volume of money is increased that amount; but for every dollar in bonds of the United States there are many, many times more bank created new deposits on their books. It is true that Government bonds, to a small degree, create Reserve funds, as we have shown in our story; but every time the Reserve authorities buy corporation stock, buy anything, the reserves of banks are increased dollar for dollar, and all of these reserves when converted into bank credit, which is as negotiable as your bank deposits, are five times more than the reserves.

Mr. Weiss and the large battalion of camouflagers for bankers, always ride the same old jaded nags, the government and labour.

Certainly inflation is too much money. It blows up the bag which is prices just as applying the hose to your tire inflates it. Too many dollars cheapen dollars.

The crime of it all is that every bank-created dollar is a counterfeit, phoney dollar, given respectability by the Congress passing the infamous Reserve Act. Except for this fact there is no reason why counterfeiters should not be given full leeway; for certainly, until a banker spots a counterfeit dollar, it circulates, paying bills, doing just as good service as the Treasury Certificate; but, should that be granted, all of us would quit work and begin printing counterfeit bills — the Reserve Act legalized counterfeiting by commercial and Reserve banks; and they fight counterfeiters because they don't want competition.

When Congress takes back the issuing of money and regulates its value, all of this inflation of money will disappear, for the constant effort of Congress will be to keep the volume of money and the volume of business of the nation in lockstep. Fight, dear reader, every attempt of anyone to lay inflation on the Government or labour. Should Congress direct the Treasurer to give it credit on the books of the Treasury for 10 million dollars it would create new money.

The same step has been taken under the Reserve system; but under the Reserve system the Congress ordered the Treasurer to engrave and turn over to the banks an equal amount of bonds free! Double, or nothing with bankers.

There is now and ought to be just one sort of money, deposits; and the Congress should take over, aggregate those deposits of whatever kind, and squeeze the phoney dollars out until the volume of deposits would be equivalent to the total business done in the current year. That would regulate the value of the dollar, of money, and only that would fix the value of money. Weiss pleads with labour to "give of itself," and complains that an engineer got full-day pay for just turning an electric switch in the morning and turning it off in the afternoon. Of course the engineer just left and went fishing He didn't, of course, have to be there every moment that he might take over if a fuse were blown, or some other mishap stopped the electric motor.

On how many days does Mr. Weiss now as Professor, and when he was a vice-president at Macy's go to his office, nod to the secretary, sign a couple of letters, get up and walk around until time to join his buddies in a golf game-rarely do these *big* fellows go to their offices before 11:00 a.m., and stay later than 1 p.m., yet when they see a workman who is not frantically working, they whine that that fellow is "featherbedding."

No give us a sound, controlled-in-volume money, and the labouring people will not have to plead and strike year in and year out, because then the dollar they get will buy the same tomorrow it bought today, and when that is true labourers are happy, and have no mind to strike. But when you pay them off with a phoney dollar that grows cheaper and cheaper as the days go by, and buys less and less, they must have more or starve. Who is to blame? The money changer, the private corporation, that godless, soulless, conscienceless "person" the Supreme Court foisted upon us, specifically The Federal Reserve System, which includes every commercial bank and deposit keeping institution in the Nation.

You could not compel them to disgorge those hundreds of billions of dollars, so long as you legalize their rapacity. The law must be repealed. All U.S. Bonds must be destroyed, and never engrave another, and Congress *must* issue our money and regulate its value ... for the Constitution recognizes no other agency of the Government, and makes no provision for Congress to re-delegate that great and important function of Government to corporations.

Read Josiah Stamp's utterances again, and then if "you want to continue the slaves of bankers and pay the cost of your own slavery," let Congress continue to legalize the crimes of banking. Since we have shown that every dollar created by Reserve and commercial banks is a phoney, counterfeit dollar, then their adding new deposit dollars to the volume of money is as much a crime as the printing by a person counterfeit bills. Our courts here, in quick order, just a few days ago convicted two printers, and the wife of one of counterfeiting Reserve notes, and circulating a few of them in Texas; yet we legalize the Federal Reserve banks and commercial banks to add counterfeit dollars to our volume of money in a constant torrent.

Seems sort of unjust to send the little printer, who was too expert at printing, to federal prison because he printed a few bills; and let his crippled brother and wife out under suspended sentences, while the five children of the head counterfeiter were torn from their parents and sent to an orphans' home, while this *big* corporation has committed the same sin millions of times, and not only goes scot free, but its deeds are dignified and legalized by *our* Congress, who each and severally took an oath to support, uphold, and defend the Constitution of the United States; yet perjured themselves by violating that same Constitution when they gave banking corporation the power to coin money and regulate the value thereof.

How long, oh, how long, gentle reader, are we going to permit Congress to do this criminal thing, and refuse to compel them to take back that Constitutional power they unconstitutionally gave to the banking; corporations?

"Banking was conceived in iniquity and born in sin."

CHAPTER XIX

MONEY IN THE ATOMIC AGE

Dear Reader: Let me emphasize, in the beginning of this chapter, that just as with our daily lives, money has passed the "horse and buggy days." Therefore, we must change completely our conception of money; forget the substance we have been calling money; forget all we have read about, the standard of value, of the gold standard; of the silver ratio; of the national credit ... all of it must be junked. We must cease to think of bills, coins, even personal cheques as assets.

Ridiculously Absurd, Stupid Nonsense...

The following House Resolution (64), adopted June 27, 1957, and inserted in the Appendix of the Record, August 30, 1957, by that erudite, intrepid Senator, Paul H. Douglas, is the most astounding admission by the Congress wholly responsible for the danger.

The first "Whereas" shouts: "... the problem of inflation is national in scope, and poses the danger of destroying our economic system, and with the failure of such system, the Nation itself; and

"Whereas the scope of the problem is too broad for anyone State to solve; and "Whereas the consumer price index has gone up 3.4 points in the past 12 months...: and

"Whereas in addition to other causes, the swollen national budget, through increased spending, will result in more inflation; and

"Whereas *Government* spending is a prime cause of inflation in that spending does not increase the Nation's productivity... Therefore be it resolved... That it is the sense of this house that the Congress of the United States should establish a commission to study all aspects of the inflation problem... That Congress should curtail spending so as to lessen the outlay of money... and that the Commission shall make recommendations to the next Congress for means and methods of curbing the inflational spiral..."

Well, general reader, let me comment on the solution NOW. If Congress will follow our suggested solution, outlaw banking, divorce the people's money from the stock market gambling, and resume their Constitutional mandate "To coin money and regulate the value thereof," the whole inflation business will be forever relegated to the limbo of "gold standard," "sound currency," and other ought-to-be-forgotten rubbish in the money realm.

But, don't forget that the hand of the Federal Reserve System penned that bunch of "whereases," and is seeking another "commission." Remember that the bankers, who have been the same since the Reserve Act in 1913 as they were for four hundred years theretofore, pulled the "near destruction" of our "nation" in the 90's, called for a "commission," which 10 years later came up with the *Reserve Act*.

And don't forget that with all that Congress could give them for giving us a "sound currency," it took them only 16 years to "bust nationwide." And they did this, not of necessity, but that they might kick out a semblance of "soundness" "gold as a basis of bank reserves," (because they could not control gold, it's coming and going) and substituted "corporation stock," which they could manipulate at will and readily to their own benefit.

This new commission has a joker up the banker's sleeve, and when they pull it, this will be a nation of the extremely rich and extremely poor. Less than 5 percent of the people will own the nation's material wealth, and employ as many of the remaining 170 million people as they need to man their giant tractors and manipulate their vast hives of industry, and the rest of us will be put on a dole, and spurned because we are so worthless and indecent as to "beg" our government for a crumb of bread.

But let me give the lie again and again to the assertion that inflation is a product of government spending. Government spending has no influence whatever on the volume of money, which is inflation; for it is merely spending taxes and revenues the people paid into the Government that "their" Government might pay its running expenses. It is the normal, beneficent, life-giving flow of deposits from buyer to seller.

Even its 90-, 180-, and 365-day current deficit borrowing has little influence on inflation; but it does inflate the bankers' coffers, because it takes 143 dollars now to pay the interest on the same amount of deficit money as it took in the 30's ...or our dollar we use to pay interest to the bankers of these short-time notes is now a 7 mills (not 100 cents) dollar.

The Government is, criminal in leaving in the hands of the Bankers U.S. Bonds, for as often as they buy one from the people, they give new deposits for them, and these new deposits create new reserves for the banks, which increase their bank credit by five times the value of the bond. There you have inflation: first the value of the bond, then the bank credit which is five times the new deposits paid for the bond.

The "nigger in the woodpile, reader, is the purchases of corporation stock on the open markets of the vast ocean of corporation stock. And the day-to-day purchase of "investment obligations," which create new deposits, adding to the volume of money constantly. But, that is not the half of it: every time a banker lends a person $50 (or less or more), a firm $500 (or less or more), or a corporation $10 million (or less or more), it adds the face of the loan to the then volume of deposits, increasing the total volume the face of the loan. These run into the trillions of dollars... and *there is, inflation.*

Too much money is inflation. Government spending is not to blame, labours' wages is not to blame. High prices is not inflation. High wages is not inflation. All are the result of cheap money, and cheap money is always the result of too much... German marks of the 20s, an instance. The lack "of gold content" has, nothing to do with it. Lack of faith of the people in it has nothing to do with it — there is just too much of it.

So long as the people have faith in their Government (and Congress may keep that faith or barter it away) our money, if in the hands of Congress, and its volume kept in lockstep with our national business demands, a deposit in the Depository, evidenced by a personal cheque, will be GOOD money, and no seller will question it, if he knows that the giver of the cheque has the deposits to cover it allocated to that particular cheque. And that is what the seller will know with our "Treasury-Personal Cheque," as, outlined in our solution of our monetary wrongs.

And this final word: when you read about "dangers to our monetary system," remember the banker is alarmed and what he means is, "We fear that we are going to lose OUR FEDERAL RESERVE SYSTEM." That is the economic system they are worried about.

I wish I knew the trillions of deposits which have been "created" (added to the volume of deposits) since 1934! And, whatever it is, the whole of it is still intact, for bankers have no way (except through bursting banks) of writing them off. The 1939 Reserve book says "deposits tend to cancel out," but they never give an example when deposits were cancelled out; but those of you who had deposits in a busted bank know that that is a very direct and effective way to "cancel them out," and that you had no recourse... you took your loss and liked it; and wonder of wonders, you have continued to have "faith" in the men who robbed you and probably refer to him as "our most respectable citizen." Won't you ever learn? May God have pity on your soul, if you continue in ignorance of this crime perpetrated against you hourly, daily, yearly — on and on.

We must drop the word banking, and disassociate money from capital and surplus. We must cease to play liabilities against assets in the realm of money. We must wipe the money slate clean, and ventilate our mental processes, that we may grasp, not what money is, but what service it shall in the future render man; for it must be man's servant and not his master.

It must not be something that is convertible into other substances, or convertible therefrom. It must have a value, and this value must be arbitrarily fixed; not on basis of gold or silver, or other material thing; but upon the work that it has to do. We must keep the dollar as the unit, but we must not escape the service that money is to perform... we must let the idea take possession of us, master us" convince us that it can and must perform that service.

Long ago when man first began to use money, he did it that he might have something, then a substance, to serve as a medium of exchange. Until he found that something, he was left to barter in the exchange of his surplus commodities for others' surplus commodities. Then even barter was confined to members of 'the same or nearby clans. Iron, shells, and many other substances were used, but as the exchange of surplus products increased and the distance between those making the exchanges grew greater and still greater, and the seller did not know the buyer, the Government stepped in and took over the manufacturing of the coins. When men began to write, the buyer began to give the seller his written promise to pay the seller for the goods at some later time; and in the meantime, the seller found others who knew the giver of the note, who were willing to accept the note for goods the note holder wanted.

Then followed paper money; but there was always in the minds of the sellers that the giver of the note, even with the government's, endorsement, might dishonour the note. Then the middle ages, during the Crusades, brought the goldsmiths into the picture; and they began to issue certificates against the gold and silverware of those leaving on a crusade; and out of this grew modern banking.

When our nation was launched under the Constitution, paper money was under great disfavour, and silver and gold coin had come into extensive use; so the Constitution provided that the "Congress should have the power to coin money, and regulate the value thereof." As proof that they had but one conception of money, and that was that it was a medium of exchange, in the same sentence it couched the power to coin money, the Constitution provided (and) "... fix the standard of weights and measures."

Franklin, Alexander Hamilton, Robert Morris, and James Madison, among the signatories to this great document, knew that only gold and silver would inspire confidence in the minds of the people; and that even with a gold-content dollar, its ultimate value was the quantity of goods it would buy; hence they placed under the one power to coin money, the power of making uniform the weights and measures of goods. That effecting the exchange of goods would be the prime purpose of money. They never dreamed that we would have a debt dollar; they would have fled from the very

SILAS WALTER ADAMS

thought of basing the volume of money on corporation stock, or the whims of 19 citizens.

Like King Henry turning to another religion that he might divorce a wife and take another, in the evil act he opened the way to protestantism, a great service to mankind, in the opinion of protestants; so in the creating of the Federal Reserve System, at the behest of bankers, in 1913, great good has come out of all of its evil, because they have fully shown that you do not need gold, or silver, or even material assets as a basis of "creating" money; you may do it in simple bookkeeping.

Not the type of money they have given us — the ocean of the evil debt-dollars - but the mechanics of money they have perfected, with some trimming away of non-essential steps, opens the way to us for the best money system on earth.

Now let's take a frank look at 'the need for money. In the vast expanse of the world, today, people are busy producing goods, offering them in the markets of the world, in the raw form, in the semi-fabricated form, and in the final manufactured form; in all stages, offered for sale.

All that they offer for sale is a surplus, goods they have produced and which they do not wish to use themselves. All of this totals great mountains of the products of the labours of man, and that these surpluses may reach users, and the users' money may return to them that they may buy from other producers goods they need and desire, there must be a something that one may hold as evidence — we call that something money.

Every person who touches these goods from the time of planting the seed, or going into the forests and mines and taking the raw material, until they are in the hands of consumers, users of these goods, adds a value; for a true value is the labour that man puts into goods before they reach the consumer. That is the goods' value. That measures the value of money; and not the other way around, as we have been taught.

Since we have been unable to ascertain that exact value as applied to all production, with service added therein, man has been forced to take some commodity as a basis. He has been in the night of his being, from the stone age to the atomic age, so he took gold. But gold no longer can meet the demands of money. It is too heavy to send from buyer to seller; it is too dangerous to expose gold to thieves. Even its quantity dwarfs, into a puny supply, when you take into consideration the world's needed supply of money; so long ago man during the horse-and-buggy days, began to print paper bills that he might have 25 or 50 times more "money" than he could get hold of in gold. And this failed, because the few billions of paper money could not shuttle back and forth between buyer and seller. Then came the personal cheque. The bills and coins now could sleep snugly in bank vaults, while the buyer mailed the seller in a distant city his cheque to cover the costs of goods which he had bought. The cheque might be for $5.00 or any amount, $5,000 or more, if he had that amount to his credit in the bank. Three cents would take the cheque to the seller, his bank gave him credit for it, the bank sent it to its Reserve Bank, the Reserve Bank credited the seller's bank with say $5,000 in its reserve fund, then it went to the Reserve Bank of the buyer's bank, and this Reserve Bank debited the buyer's bank reserve account $5,000, and the Reserve Bank sent the cheque to the buyer's bank, and his account was debited $5,000.

And the only material thing that made the rounds was a small piece of paper, a personal cheque. Other than the cost of bookkeeping, the debiting and crediting of the $5,000 on four different books, the entire cost was the postage, which amounted to 12 cents.

Under our proposed plan, both the Reserve Banks would be eliminated, and the seller's bank would credit the seller's account $5,000, and the buyer's bank would debit his account $5,000. Could you desire a more fluid money? Could you devise a simpler way of keeping track of the money of the nation as it shuttled back and forth between buyer and seller? Could you wish for a safer method of keeping your money, the country's money?

But I have gone a bit ahead of my story. We have shown that money is intangible. We have shown that it is an evidence that man had produced a surplus of goods. That it is an evidence kept on the books of banks. That it can be transferred from one depositor's account to another's account in remote cities, simply on a written order from the buyer to the seller, made through a personal cheque, mailed to seller.

The goods which may have been consumed and now non-existent, and only the goods are the bases of the deposit credits — of money. You need no gold reserves, no chattels, no "securities." The figures on the books of the banks, when placed there only to the credit of the producers of goods, ought to be the only visible form of the billions of dollars which may appear on the books of the banks to the credit of the people - or that would have been true, if the Congress had obeyed the Constitution and kept the power to create money, regulate the value thereof, and of foreign coin (in terms of our own).

What I have been leading up to is this fact:

Money is figures on the books of banks, to the credit of the people who have sold surplus goods, and service, and the only visible form of this money is personal cheques, and currency.

If the Congress will take back the creation and control of money, keep the deposit accounts of the people, and squeeze all of the debt-dollars out, and permit no dollar to appear on the books of the depositories, except a dollar earned by the production of goods; then our money will be the soundest money on earth.

So long as a person holds a deposit dollar on the books of the depositories, that means that he has sold surplus goods or services to that amount more than he has consumed; and as often as a person exhausts his deposits, it means another or others have surrendered to him an equal amount of goods to the goods he had formerly surrendered.

This will make an endless, unbroken chain, links added as production increased, links (dollars) ever increasing as products increase.

Forget all that you have thought you knew about money; forget the school book definitions of money. Just remember that it is "an evidence" that surplus goods and labour have been produced and rendered.

Forget bills, forget coins, remember they have not the least relationship to money, any more than your unsigned personal cheque; that your personal cheque, when properly filled in and signed, if you have deposits in the bank to cover, is just as good money as bills and coins.

Always when you think of money, think of figures on the books of banks, now; please, God, it may soon be the books of U.S. Depositories.

Had Congress taken over money in 1934, instead of giving the bankers almost unlimited power over money and the nation's credit, there would not be $272,000,000,000 U.S. Bonds drawing $10 billion interest (taxes) a year; and there would not be a trillion in personal accounts, in competition with our personal earned dollar, making it a 20-cent dollar as against a 100-cent dollar of the thirties.

I have made these explanations because writers always stress currency (coin and bills) in their money discussions. You must place currency and personal cheques in the same category. Each is an instrument you may use in paying for goods or services. Each is convertible into deposits; and deposits are convertible into cash or personal cheques. But the personal cheque always takes the lead. If you have deposits, and wish to convert them into cash, you must write a cheque against your deposits, surrender it to the banker, and he will hand you the cash; or if you have cash and wish to convert it into deposits, you may hand it to the banker and he will hand you a deposit slip, showing that you have had your deposits credited with the cash you surrendered.

I want you to forget all forms of money but the figures on the books of banks; then when I talk about a debt dollar, or an earned dollar, you can get the difference. An earned dollar is one you get when you serve someone, or sell some product of your labour, or some product you have come into possession of. A debt dollar is a dollar you came into possession of when you borrow from a banker, not a loan shark, or a person who must give you the cash or his cheque against his deposits. All dollars created when bankers buy notes, mortgages, and other investment obligations, or lend you on your personal note, are debt dollars. These are the dollars we must destroy, and prevent their ever being issued again.

What Treasury Depositories Will Accomplish

When we eliminate the debt dollar, we will eliminate fluctuating prices, eliminate the fellow who comes in with his debt dollar to compete with you in the markets of the world. Returning to the earned dollar will wipe out all national debts, all debt dollars, and destroy the army of people who live off the cream of the earth and never serve anyone or produce anything.

But the man willing to work and produce, or serve others, will prosper as never before.

It will end wars, it will end hunger and want, it will put us in lock-step with the atomic age.

It will end great fortunes, and debt money cannot come into a community and build great trade emporiums not needed, and destroy the businesses of those who serve in the retailing of goods: on a modest basis. It will not handicap needed industry, but will protect it from the exploitation of the debt dollar creators.

It is a far cry from the "coining of silver and gold coin" for money, to the flood of debt dollars the banks are flooding the country with, hourly, daily, monthly, year in and year out.

Then your insurance premium will not bounce higher, while your insurance policy skids lower and lower. Then your savings will not be cut in half, to one-third, aye, to one-fourth, as now. It will mean, when our earned dollars as evidenced on the books of the depositories are controlled and limited in volume to the surplus goods produced and consumed, that your dollar will buy the same quantity in 1997 it buys in 1957. Stability, soundness, elasticity, and confidence will tincture every American dollar.

Perhaps we can see the injustice of our present debt dollar by taking the simplest unit of people, the family.

Let's take the proverbial family of nine, the parents and seven sons. All working together can easily produce an abundance of needed food, clothing and shelter; but four of the sons, the eldest and strongest, decide they will quit work, dress well, spend their time leisurely enjoying reading, travelling, or just loafing.

The other five then must do the work of the nine. That means that to enjoy the same abundance, they must work four-fifths longer hours. When all were working they could easily do all of the work in 10 hours, but now the five must work 18 hours a day, to meet the accustomed plenty.

But they can't work that many hours daily. Human strength will not let them do that, so they struggle 12 hours daily, and fail to fill the barns and store houses as before.

But the four well-dressed, soft-handed brothers write debt dollars, and buy the products their brothers and parents have produced, leaving the producers an insufficient supply. The older sons of other families seeing this easy life for the strong, begin the same practice. Meeting often in their leisure, they discussed among themselves their great advantage. They decide to open an office, let this office issue debt dollars, and have some system about it, to the end that the sons of one family could buy surpluses of other families, and because there was no limit to the amount of debt dollars they could pile up, soon the working, producing members of the families found that the debt dollar they got for their goods would not buy as many goods as they had surrendered to their loafing neighbours for their debt dollars, and the weaker families soon had to go back to a full family working at the difficult task of producing a living.

The issuing of corporation stock is one of the greatest sins in this field of debt dollars. You as an individual, wish to enlarge your business, and you borrow from the money lenders money to do this. You mortgage all your assets as security. You must pay heavy interest, whether you make a profit on your business or not, and should you fail within 18 months to pay the note in full, you would be brought into court, and the lender would take your property, your business away from you and other assets.

But when the corporation wants to expand its business it issues more stock certificates, but gives no mortgage, and puts, them on the market. The Reserve Banks, or the City National Bank of New York, buys the stock. They put it on the stock exchanges, and suckers buy them as an "investment," and the corporation uses this money, oftentimes just to increase their luxuries and not their business facilities.

The corporation has issued a strange form of note to get the money. It is supposed to draw interest, but may never pay a dividend. Should the corporation fail as the small business man did, the holders of these corporation stocks could not sue and receive their money; they would have in their hands worthless notes un-collectable through the courts.

But in each instance debt dollars were created and added to the money supply, and these debt dollars remained to cheapen the earned dollar.

Take from the bankers, all money lenders the power to add debt dollars to our money supply, and you will make it impossible for a few to not only own the material wealth, but the production and the manpower of the nation. It will make it impossible for a man, within a few years to rise from poverty to assets running into the millions. Throughout the United States, those who enjoy the creation of debt dollars are using this almost worthless money to buy all property. Our lands are passing rapidly into the hands of a few. Our industries are being consolidated into the hands of a few. Men speak of their 85,000-acre ranches... contractors boast of having a half billion contracts to build great dams or to do other works of magnitude. All of this, while the toiling, working, suffering masses struggle for a bare subsistence. The small business man is rapidly being crowded out. The small farmers are being driven from their farms. The small industries are being consolidated under a few giant corporations. The duPonts, as a horrible example, not only control the productions of arms and ammunition, extensive industrial corporations, but are deep in the banking business, the business of issuing billions of debt dollars and using them to buy up the resources of the Nation — and all the time fomenting wars because wars, as nothing else, make billionaires.

Congressman Patman quoted in the Congressional Record, a few days ago said: "I believe it was Lenin who said... when asked why America did not go

Communistic, that as long as America has a system wherein so many people are engaged in small business and have a stake in their economy the country will never go Communistic."

Our ocean of debt dollars, dollars secured through corporation stock which the corporations will never pay for... they get the debt dollar, and continue to enjoy its power and profit, but they don't have to worry about the repayment of those notes, as the small business man must worry; this will drown us.

The Government builds great dams, makes possible thousands of acres of irrigated fertile land, but these acres have been bought up before the dam is well started by the men with debt dollars in the billions, and the family who might improve its living standards on 50 or 75 acres must stay in the hinterland, and corporations farm with big tractors and few labourers, blocks of a thousand acres. And their products compete with the little man's products.

The oil man with gold flowing from inexpensive holes in the ground, take their billions and go out and buy up hundreds of thousands of acres of land, driving the small farmers off the land, into the cities to become burdens on the backs of the rest of the producers.

The Nation's bankers are busy destroying labour unions, the working man's only means of fighting for a decent wage, and entering into even union elections ...couple this with the debt dollar's dispossessing the property holders, and you put our government completely in the hands of the debt dollar few. That means that by legislation they will have complete control.

They gave us a 7 -Mills Dollar for a 100-Cent Dollar Quoting Congressman Patman again, in the Congressional Record, April 30, 1957:

"Now let us take the value of money today. They talk about a dollar going down to 50 cents. For certain purposes it has gone down to 7 mills. Imagine a dollar worth (only) 7 mills. That is exactly right. If you measure the value of a dollar in interest that was paid by the Government in 1939 on 90-day Treasury bills; with the interest that is paid today on 90-day Treasury bills, you will discover that to be a fact. It is really astounding. It is really shocking. Yesterday the newspapers would not carry it because they thought there was something wrong about it.

There is nothing wrong about it. You pay $143 today for interest on the same amount of money on Treasury bills, for the same length of time, that you paid only $1 for in 1939. There is the value of a dollar sinking from $1 in 1939, for the purpose of paying interest on 90-day Treasury certificates, to 7 mills in April, 1957. "Furthermore, the value of the dollar on prime commercial paper, 4 and 6 months - that is also very disturbing — is only worth 16.3 cents. That is all it is worth for purposes of paying interest on prime commercial paper, 4 to 6 months. It is worth about one-sixth of what it was worth in 1939."

There you have the bankers' debt dollar in its naked setting. There you have a crime laid at its door, an ugly sin. If the Treasury must pay with such a cheap dollar; if the best borrowers have to pay with a 16-cent dollar; then try to imagine what the husband who must borrow on 30 days must pay for $100, he must have if his children eat.

The astounding thing about Mr. Patman is the fact that he ferrets out and makes public these astounding crimes of banking, yet he insists that we have the greatest banking system on earth. He even admits, asserts that the banks pay nothing for these Treasury bills, the notes and mortgages of the people. He asks, "What do they pay for those notes? They do not pay anything. This is one of the powers we (Congress) have granted to them, the power to create money, and they use that money to buy our government bonds.

They hold the bonds and continue to draw interest on "them!"

Then he laments, "That is the reason we have let the Federal Reserve System get away from Congress. The Federal Reserve System does not come back to Congress for an appropriation every year. It is the only agency of the Government that we have in our country that does not depend or rely upon Congress for anything. We have delegated to them enough power and credit where they buy our Government bonds, hold the bonds," collect interest running into the billions a year.

Why should the people submit to this criminal thing? Why should we turn over the nation's credit, its power to coin money, to private corporations, then turn arouncl and borrow that credit at a cost of billions a year in interest, in addition to giving them the principal in U.S. Bonds?

Think of a Congressman who has been there years, lamenting that the Government has no control over the banks. That the Government must borrow money on short 90-day time. Then, who is master of the Nation? Congress? Certainly not. The bankers have a death grip on our throats, and we ignorantly don't know whose hand is there. Think of a 1939 dollar being worth only 7 mills today when Uncle Sam pays interest to these money thieves.

In 1943 Mr. Patman said: "Federal Reserve Banks are federal in name only. The Government does not own one penny of stock in them." In 1957, after being brainwashed as chairman of the money and banking committee of Congress, he said, "This you can put down as an absolute fact — that the Federal Reserve banking system (that includes, 14,357 commercial banks) is not owned by the private banks. It is owned by the Government of the United States."

Can you imagine anything more ludicrous? If you had $5,000 in the bank, and needed $50 for a few days, would you pay the bank 143 times what you would have had to pay in 1939 for the use of your own money? That is what the Government is doing through the ignorant, under duress Congressmen. They have given the Reserve System the power to do this. Then we are slaves of the bankers. Our government is the slave of the bankers.

But to make Mr. Patman's position the ultimate in absurdity, he says, "The Constitution is very plain that Congress shall have all power over money, but, obviously, Congress cannot administer that power. So Congress delegated it to the Federal Reserve System ..."

Why didn't Congress delegate it to the Treasury of the United States, and keep a close rein over it?

What is there difficult about money that makes it impossible for Congress to control it? There is nothing but the crooked control of money by bankers. There are but two problems which would confront Congress: (a) the creation of new deposits as often as business needed them; and

(b) the keeping of the people's deposits, cashing and clearing their cheques. So simple that a graduate from a high school business course could do it.

Had Congress delegated this, work to the Treasury, when it needed ready cash and there were no funds in its tax balance, Congress would have ordered the Treasury to give the Government credit for the additional money needed, and there would have been no U.S. Bonds hanging over the rest of us from there on out, and the billions we are paying bankers for the privilege of using our own credit could go into better living for all of us.

Every time the Government or any private institution or person borrows money under the Reserve Banking System, new debt dollars are added to our money supply, to cheapen our earned dollars, and they, like

U.S. Bonds hang on years and years, taking billions of interest money out of our pockets, hundreds of billions, each year.

Finally, let me quote the then second richest man in Great Britain, and at that time the top banker of the world, Sir Josiah Stamp:

"Banking was conceived in iniquity and born in sin... The bankers own the earth; take it away from them but leave them the power to create money, and with the flick of the pen (debt dollars) they will create enough money to buy it back again... Take this power away from them, and all great fortunes like mine will disappear, and they ought to disappear, because this would be a better and a happier world to live in... But, if you want to continue the slaves of bankers, and pay the cost of your own slavery, let them continue to create money and control credit."

Then go back to 150 years ago when the founder of international banking, Rothschild, said: "Let me create a nation's money and I care not who writes its laws."

Pass this book on to your neighbour; better, sell him a copy, and let's inform the people of the United States on the crimes being daily committed in the name of money, and compel Congress to take back the "coining of money and the regulating the value thereof."

May This Dream Forever be the Dream of the Poor in the World Let me follow the last page of this book with this apostrophe to the suffering throughout the world — this dream the rest of the world has dreamed in anticipation and yearning that they, too might gain entrance into the United States of America — a dream that was beautifully unfolding until we began to draw about us the selfish robe of nationalism.

The most American way of life is to hear every man's story, put all of them in our mental mortars, bray them well with the pestle of thought, spread the compound thin on the mortar board, and then cut out a new pattern of life. The truest American way of life is carved on the Statue of Liberty:

Give me your tired, your poor,
Your huddled masses yearning to breathe free,
The wretched refuse of your teeming shore.
Send these, the homeless, tempest-tossed, to me:
I lift my lamp beside the golden door.
— Emma Lazarus.

These have come and been cast into our melting pot, been fused into our blood, annealing muscle, sinew and bone, begetting physical form of beauty, strength and courage, temples of intellect that have astounded the world with their vision and creative thinking, delving into the most minute recesses of matter and projecting man, encumbered with tons of steel into the rarefied stratospheres, where Taurus in the light of the Moon, tips to his lips the Great Dipper, as he drinks a toast to the Pleiades; as they ride in the chariot of Night along the etherial Milky Way!

That this dream may ever beckon the homeless, tempest-tossed, huddled masses from every teeming shore, is the sincere wishes of the Author.

"We shall nobly save or meanly lose the last best hope of earth." — *Abraham Lincoln.*

These Facts Alone Should Outlaw Banking.

The Whole Story of the Creation of New Deposits

The following quotation is lifted from the 1939 Edition of *The Federal Reserve System — Its Purposes and Functions.*

Page 70, Paragraph 3: Realizing that any additional loans it (the member bank) made would increase its deposits out of proportion to its reserves, the commercial bank might stop making new loans. Suppose, however, that the Reserve authorities were of the opinion more loans might advantageously be made and that the bank should be provided with additional reserves so that it could make them. Suppose they therefore purchased $20,000,000 of securities in the open market. The seller of the securities would deposit in the commercial bank the money (the Reserve authorities' check against no funds) they received in payment. The commercial bank in turn would deposit it (the seller's cheque received from the Reserve authorities) in its reserve account in the Reserve Bank. Having these additional reserves of $20,000,000, the commercial bank, by making loans, could increase its deposits to five (or maybe seven times) as much or $100,000,000 — the $20,000,000 being the 20 percent reserves required against deposits of $100,000,000! End of quote The parenthesis enclose my explanatory statements. — S.W. Adams, author of "The Legalized Crime of Banking."

The Reserve authorities may do this without consulting the bank. Too, you will note that the Reserve authorities' cheque "created" two $20 million funds, and the third created $100 million:

(a) it created for the seller of the securities $20 million bank deposits, subject to cheque; (b) then it went to the Reserve Bank to clear, and "created" $20,000,000 bank reserves to the credit of the commercial bank, and it could have demanded $20,000,000 in cash, but, of course, it didn't do that, so it left it there to the credit of its account; then the commercial bank too credit on its own books $100 million bank credit. This they used to make loans to customers, or to buy investment obligations - mortgages, promissory notes, debentures, deeds of trust, corporation stock, et cetera. In making loans and in buying investments obligations, they converted the $100 million into bank deposits, subject to cheque wherewith "business men and other persons make the bulk of their monetary payments." Adding the $20 million the stock seller deposited in his bank, and we have added in new money to our money supply $120 million! And in addition to that the commercial bank holds $100 million in notes, mortgages and other investment obligations, which increases our monetary fund another $100 million, making a grand total of $220 million monetary values, which grew out of the Reserve authorities buying only $20 million corporation stock.

And remember the Reserve authorities wrote a cheque against no funds, which would make it a hot cheque if you wrote one against no funds, so the $20 million of corporation stock became the property of the Federal Reserve Corporation, gratis, the $100 million of bank credit became the property of the commercial *bank, gratis, which it used to buy* $100 *million of investment obligations; and when the commercial bank collected all notes, or resold all corporation stock they may have bought, the banker had* $100 *million plus interest, less cost of doing business, gratis — and not a penny cost the bank one thin dime!*

"We boast of having liberated four million slaves, but we are careful to conceal the ugly fact that by our iniquitous monetary system, we have nationalized a system of oppression more refined but none the less cruel than the old system of chattel slavery." — Horace Greeley on the passage of the National Banking Act, 1873.

So you can easily see how they can build great bank buildings, motor bank annexes, and buy interest in endless corporations — briefly how they can buy the earth with a flick of the pen. And don't forget that when reserves were dependent on new gold, either from domestic mines or from foreign countries, the bankers had little control over the movement of gold; and, too it was always limited. When they demonetized gold in 1934, and made the purchase of corporation stock the basis of bank reserves, the sky became the limit. The only limitation on the creation of new bank reserves, as shown above, are the whims of the Reserve authorities, consisting of nineteen members — the seven members of the Board of Governors of the Federal Reserve System, and the presidents of the twelve Reserve banks.

The Pauper and the Rich Man

The pauper (the Federal Reserve Bank) with assets of $52 billion with no productive know how, and less than 100,000 stockholders, loaned the rich man (The United States Government) with well over $350 billion in physical assets plus $250 billion in productive capacity and know- how, with 170 million stockholders, $300 billion to fight World War II.

Can you imagine the greatest corporation on earth, with 170 million stockholders and assets running over $600 billion, turning to a corporation with less than 100,000 stockholders and assets of only $52 billion to borrow money? Can you imagine Rockefeller saying to his chauffer: "Tom, I am transferring my personal chequeing account, which is around $1 billion, to your account. You may spend it as you please, provided that when I need some cash, you will hand it to me. Of course, I will give you my note for cash I receive and pay interest on the note." Well, that is exactly what Congress did in 1913 when it passed the Reserve Act. To fight World War II, we gave the bankers of the United States $300 billion in U.S. Bonds that we might use the Nation's credit. In addition, we permitted them to take a credit of $300 billion in their reserve accounts. This gave then $2 trillion 100 billion bank credit. These credits are to bankers what your deposit credits on their books are to you. They can lend it, or buy investment obligations — it is cash to them!

So adding the $300 billion in Bonds to their bank credit, we find that the bankers (the then paupers) came out of World War II $2 trillion 400 billion richer than when we went into the War.

The United States' Government (the then rich man), thanks to the stupidity and venality of her sons (congressmen), and newspapers and journals, came out of the War $300 billion in debt! And, dear reader, that fable happens to be true.

If interested, and want to know how this crime may be punished and the practice stopped, write

S.W. Adams, 2004 South First St., Austin 4, Texas, and place your order for his book, "The Legalized Crime of Banking," and a "Suggested Solution."

The End.

GLOSSARY

1. *Reserve Act of* 1913-Created Federal Reserve System by which Congress abdicated its Constitutional authority to create money and control credit, turning this important function of Government over to private corporations.

2. *Reserve Act of* 1934 — Demonetized gold, substituted Corporation stock as standard of money. Raised price of monetary gold from $25.67 an ounce to $35 an ounce, and outlawed the selling of gold to other than the Government, and made it illegal for a person to have gold coin or bullion, except that which he bought from the Government to be used in his arts; making it compulsory that the Government buy all gold mined in the United States, or sent to the United States.

3. *Reserve Act of* 1957 — Greatly extended powers of Reserve authorities.

4. *Federal Reserve System* — Twelve Federal Reserve Banks and some 14,000 member commercial banks, trust companies and savings institutions, combined into a giant private corporation with the power to issue all money, create all deposits, and control the credit of the nation — it holds the power of life or death over every person in the Nation.

5. *Reserve Board of Governors* — Seven persons appointed by the President of the United States, confirmed by the Senate, who serve 14 years. They supervise the operation of the 12 Reserve Banks, and pump money into circulation or siphon it out at their pleasure.

6. *Twelve Reserve Banks* — Each serves a district, with its branch Reserve Banks. Each is a corporation.

Member banks are their stockholders, and their principal function is to create and hold the member bank reserves, cash and clear their cheques.

7. *Reserve Open Market Committee* — Is comprised of the seven members of the Reserve Board of Governors, and five members of the Federal Reserve Banks. The committee directs the open market operations of the Federal Reserve banks, that is, the purchase and sale of Government securities, bonds, and corporation securities, stocks and bonds. The purpose of these operations is to create bank reserves, basis of bank credit, which banks use to buy investment obligations, and to make loans.

8. *Reserve Advisory Council* — Twelve members, one chosen by each district Reserve Bank, who work in conjunction with the seven members of the Board of Governors, in making policies, directing the over-all affairs of the Reserve System.

9. *Reserve Authorities* — A term applied to any group of Reserve officials when it is unnecessary to indicate which group is functioning.

10. *Member Banks* — All national banks, and such state banks and trust companies as meet requirements for membership. There are some 14,000 member commercial banks, and trust companies, and several thousand smaller banks who must function under the wing of some larger member bank.

11. *Commercial Banks* — Private corporations who carry the deposit accounts of the people, make loans and buy investment obligations. They are the contact points between the Reserve Banks and the people.

12. *Currency* — Is bills and coin engraved and minted by the Treasury to be used as cash register and pocket change.

13. *Treasury Certificates* — Are the smaller bills, ten, five and one-dollar silver certificates, redeemable in silver.

14. *United States Notes* — Under Lincoln's urgent demand, Congress ordered the Treasury to engrave approximately $350,000,000 simple promises of the Government without interest; and these notes are still in circulation, an unknown remainder of them, and they have been the best money the Nation has ever issued, and have done hundreds of billions of services with no interest costs.

15. *Gold Certificates* — The Government cannot legally issue its own gold certificates, as it did before 1934, and does in the matter of silver, but it has engraved in large denominations approximately $22 billion Reserve Gold Certificates which may not be; used in general circulation, but which transfers the title to our $22,620,251,821 gold stocks to private corporations, and these gold certificates lie in the 12 district reserve banks, which the holders could present if the crises came, and take possession of all the gold in the Treasury and in Fort Knox bullion tomb.

16. *Reserve Notes* — The Treasury has engraved over $27 billion Federal Reserve Notes for the Reserve Banks at a cost of only 30c a $1,000. These notes are used in preponderant volume in all currency circulation.

17. *Reserve Bank Notes* — The Treasury did engrave early in its history several hundred million dollars worth but discontinued that because they had to

pay a 1% interest on them; so they are rapidly retiring them. Bankers like to collect interest, but have to pay it. In 1946 the Circulation Statement shows there were $455,708,045, but the 1957 statement shows only $135,333,191 in circulation.

18. *Reserve Bank Reserves* — Funds created by the depositing of Reserve cheques by commercial banks, which had been deposited to the credit of the recipients (corporations) in their accounts, dollar for dollar.

19. *Commercial Bank Reserves* — The same figures on the books of the Reserve banks to the credit of commercial banks.

20. *Reserve Bank Credit* The unlimited power to create money, granted to them in the Reserve Act of 1913. It "consists of 'funds' they are empowered to create. The process of creation is one of giving the promise of the Reserve Banks, in the form of Reserve notes or deposits, in exchange for the promises made to other Reserve Banks."

21. *Commercial (Member) Bank Credit* — A multiple, ranging from 5 to 10 times the amount of reserves the bank holds in its reserve bank. The Board of Governors may raise or lower this requirement, making money tight or easy.

22. *Commercial Bank Deposits* — The deposits created when banks make loans or buy investment obligations, and the borrower or seller leaves his money on deposit. All deposits are created in this way, except when the Reserve authorities buy Government or corporation securities, then the deposits are created to credit of government.

23. *Personal Cheque* — A depositor's order instructing his bank to transfer funds from his account to the

recipient's account, and is used in making the bulk of their monetary payments.

24. *Legal Tender Money* — Coin and currency. On the Reserve notes there is printed this: "This note is Legal Tender for All Debt, both Public and Private and is redeemable in *lawful* money (that is by giving you another bill like the one you present) at the United States Treasury or at any Federal Reserve Bank." On U.S. Silver Certificates, it is the same except it is "redeemable in silver dollars."

25. *Investment Obligations* — *U.S.* Bonds, corporate bonds, personal notes, mortgages, debentures, bills of exchange acceptable promise to pay, anything representing a monetary value.

Loans — The extending of bank credit to borrowers, and the "purchase of investment obligations by banks is an extension of credit; therefore a loan.

Cash — Is the bills and coin bankers keep on hand to issue to depositors, to be used in over-the- counter purchases. It has no value until in the hands of a would-be buyer.

Rediscount — The buying as a discount of commercial bank investment obligations by Reserve Banks.

Acceptable Paper — Usually drafts, bills of lading held by shippers or sellers of goods while in transit.

Fiscal Agents of Government — are the Reserve Banks who hold the Government's deposits, and clear their cheques; they also serve in assisting the Government in issuing bonds and other securities.

Issuing Currency — The Treasury engraves all bills and mints all coin, but all of it is put into circulation by the Reserve Banks. All coin and Treasury certificates are deposited by the Treasury in the Reserve Banks, for which the Government gets deposit credit, but all Reserve notes and Reserve Gold Certificates are turned over to the Reserve Banks (on demand) gratis, and the Government gets no deposit credits for them.

Cashing Cheques — The depositor buys from the bank cash, paying for it by chequeing to the bank an equal amount of his deposits.

Clearing Checks — The passing of cheques drawn on one bank and deposited in another, through a "clearing house" or the Reserve Banks.

Public Debt — That sum spent by the Government above its income — now about $280 billion.